THE PEOPLE OF THE CREED

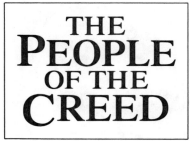

THE
PEOPLE
OF THE
CREED

The Story Behind the Early Church

ANTHONY E. GILLES

Nihil Obstat:	Rev. Hilarion Kistner, O.F.M.
	Rev. John J. Jennings
Imprimi Potest:	Rev. Jeremy Harrington, O.F.M.
	Provincial
Imprimatur:	+ James H. Garland, V.G.
	Archdiocese of Cincinnati
	January 9, 1985

The *nihil obstat* and *imprimatur* are a
declaration that a book or pamphlet is
considered to be free from doctrinal or moral
error. It is not implied that those who have
granted the *nihil obstat* and *imprimatur*
agree with the contents, opinions or
statements expressed.

Book design and cover by Julie Lonneman.

SBN 0-86716-046-2

TO EDWARD STERITI, O.C.S.O.

Other books by Anthony E. Gilles:

The People of the Book
The People of the Way
Fundamentalism: What Every Catholic Needs to Know

PREFACE

About the only thing I remember from my first encounter with Church history is a textbook illustration of Pope Leo the Great. His head was surrounded by a halo and beams of light streamed down upon him from heaven as he stood defiantly before Attila the Hun at the gates of Rome. My teacher gave the impression that Pope Leo, by turning back the Huns, had single-handedly saved Rome—and thus all future civilization—from barbarian destruction.

Why did this heroic image of Leo's stand at the gates of Rome so firmly implant itself in my mind? Probably because it so accurately reflected my view at the time—and the view of most people—that history means the "big names," the "big events," and the dates associated with them. This tendency to dramatize history and to present it only in terms of major personalities and events pervades every type of historical writing, especially histories of the Church. Church history often reads simply like the chronicle of ecclesiastical bigwigs, and we erroneously conclude that "little people," the ordinary believers, contributed nothing to the story of the Church.

As a result we get the feeling that "Church" means only bishops, popes, councils, theologians and debates about doctrine. The "Church" in this type of Church history becomes an "it," an institution separated from our everyday lives as Christians struggling to live the gospel.

Much the same dichotomy is present today between life as we experience it and the names and events that get reported on the six o'clock news. In my own parish I doubt that anyone directs more than one thought in 10 million toward the goings-on at the Vatican, or that one parishioner out of a hundred has ever heard of Karl Rahner or Hans Kung. More than likely the early Christians were not much different in this respect from today's average American Catholic. Much of what we identify today as "early Church history" would probably seem pretty removed from their everyday experiences.

I hope to avoid this pitfall and to touch base throughout with the story of the "little people" and their contribution to Church life. I want you to come away from this book thinking of Church not as an "it" but as an "us." Despite my desire to achieve this, however, I am limited by certain obstacles of which you should be made aware.

Of necessity the historian deals with the *tangible* remnants of a people's past—for example, the written records of Church councils, bishops' letters and scholars' treatises. Tangible remnants of everyday life and ordinary people are much harder to come by.

Where, then, can we look for clues to what made the early Christians "Christian," and to what drew them to the Church and kept them there? If we had to pick one word to summarize the concept of "everyday Christian life," that word would be *belief*—their shared *belief* in Jesus Christ as God-become-man.

The real story of the early Church, then, is the story of God's people and the faith which molded these people together. That story, however, is somewhat elusive. Unlike the doings of bishops and intellectuals, there is less tangible evidence available to reconstruct the shared sentiment of early Christian believers.

Our best sources for insight into the belief of the early Church are the great Creeds whose development we will plot in the chapters ahead. It is in the Creeds that we come closest to a comprehension of the early Church's belief, and to an understanding of what the early Church period was really like.

In telling this story we must of necessity refer to "big" names and events and get involved in many seemingly abstruse and complicated theological discussions. Please don't let this fact-of-historical-life deter you from realizing that the story behind the early Church is also the story of people like you and me, who tried to express in their ordinary lives the gospel's central teaching, "The Word became flesh and made his dwelling among us."

CONTENTS

INTRODUCTION

The Search for 'Something More'

The earliest Christians were Jews. Religion for the Jews, and thus for these first Christians, was a matter of *revelation*, not of philosophical speculation. Like most of us today, these first Christians relied more on faith than they did on reason.

But something altogether different happened when non-Jews started converting to Christianity. Keep in mind that most educated non-Jews in these early centuries approached religious questions from the point of view of rational, speculative analysis. That was the pervasive atmosphere of the Greco-Roman world. While Jewish Christians had been accustomed to accepting *revealed* truth through faith, non-Jewish converts expected to come to the knowledge of truth through *reason*. When these two different approaches converged in the early Church, a distinct climate of uneasiness resulted.

There is, of course, more to early Church history than this tension between faith and reason—as we shall see. Yet it would be correct to say that the distinctive feature of the first 600 years of Christianity is the Church's struggle to explain in *rational* terms the central mystery of Christian *revelation*, the incarnation: "The Word became flesh and made his dwelling among us."

What did it really mean to say that God had become a man in Jesus Christ? By what process had the incarnation occurred? What was the significance of the incarnation for ordinary human life on earth? What did the incarnation say about God and about humanity? How were Christians to live and conduct their everyday lives once the incarnation had been

1

acknowledged as the key Christian teaching? These were some of the speculative questions which the incarnation suggested to non-Jewish thinkers.

Many Christians today might ask, "Why didn't these non-Jewish rationalists just read the New Testament and believe?" First of all, remember that the New Testament writings as we have them today were not collected into a body of organized literature until about the end of the second century. Further, not until the seventh and eighth centuries did a firm consensus of opinion emerge as to what Christian writings should be included in the *authentic* New Testament. (We'll discuss this in more detail in Chapter Three.) Finally, the New Testament by and large was written from a Jewish, revelational perspective. Something more than the New Testament was needed to answer the questions which non-Jewish rationalists asked about the incarnation. The explanation of how the Church arrived at this "something more" is the key element in the story behind the early Church.

THE CREEDS: LINK BETWEEN FAITH AND REASON

Because of the two perspectives on the incarnation—the revelational and the speculative—the content of Christian belief was not always easily determined everywhere, and by everyone, during the first five centuries after the Apostles. For five centuries Christians asked themselves hard questions about the substance of their belief and put themselves to great tests to confirm that belief.

What they needed—and what the future development of the Church *required* at this early stage of its history—were short, formal, memorizable statements which summarized the essential content of Christian belief. Thus anyone—especially rationally minded non-Jews—could know without a great deal of difficulty what the key truths of Christian revelation were.

These foundational statements of normative Christian belief are called *Creeds*. The central element in our story will be how the early Church's great Creeds developed. The story of this creedal development is what distinguishes early Church history from that of later eras, so much so that the development of these Creeds can be thought of simply as the story behind the early Church.

The early Christians—through great controversy, sacrifice and struggle—earned the nickname I have given them: "People of the Creed." In recounting their story we touch the heart of the early Church and its belief. We come to that place where faith and reason harmonize, where revelation and speculation achieve a working synthesis.

2

As you might imagine, explaining how these Creeds developed is not an easy matter. In fact, it is a very complex story. In order to show how the Church through its Creeds synthesized faith and reason, revelation and speculation, we must first know at least a little about the non-Jewish systems of thought which the early Church confronted.

Not all non-Jewish thinkers thought alike. In Chapter Two we will discuss the two most prominent systems of thought which influenced the ancient world: Stoicism and Platonism. In doing so we will notice a most interesting phenomenon: As we move into the second and third centuries we find that Christians in the eastern part of the Roman Empire (who spoke Greek) tended more toward a Platonic, conceptual approach in their quest to harmonize faith and reason; in contrast, Christians in the western part of the Empire (who spoke Latin) adopted a more Stoic, practical approach. Let's take a quick look at this divergence of early Christianity into Eastern and Western branches.

EAST AND WEST:
TWO APPROACHES TO THE CHRISTIAN FAITH

First of all we must define what we mean by "East" and "West." As suggested above, one way to make this definition would be according to language. By and large, Eastern Christians spoke Greek and Western Christians Latin. Language by itself, however, would not be a satisfactory means of distinguishing between the Eastern and Western Churches. Christians in the West, for example, celebrated Mass in Greek during the second and third centuries, and most of the Western Christian writers during these centuries wrote in Greek.

Perhaps the best way to distinguish between East and West is in connection with a *political* division which took place within the Roman Empire. In the year 286 the Roman emperor Diocletian, finding the vast Empire more and more unmanageable, moved his headquarters to Nicomedia in today's Turkey. Diocletian ruled the eastern half of the Empire while his "co-Augustus," Maximian, ruled the western half of the Empire from Rome. In this division—roughly speaking—"East" and "West" lay on opposite sides of an imaginary line which we can draw due north from about the middle of North Africa up through what is today Yugoslavia (see map on p. 4).

Over a period of time the Church east of this imaginary line—again, generally speaking—began to develop thought patterns and a life-style that differed from those of the Church in the West. The Western Church was, by and large, more practical and down-to-earth in its concerns (judged at least by our own Western perspective) while the

3

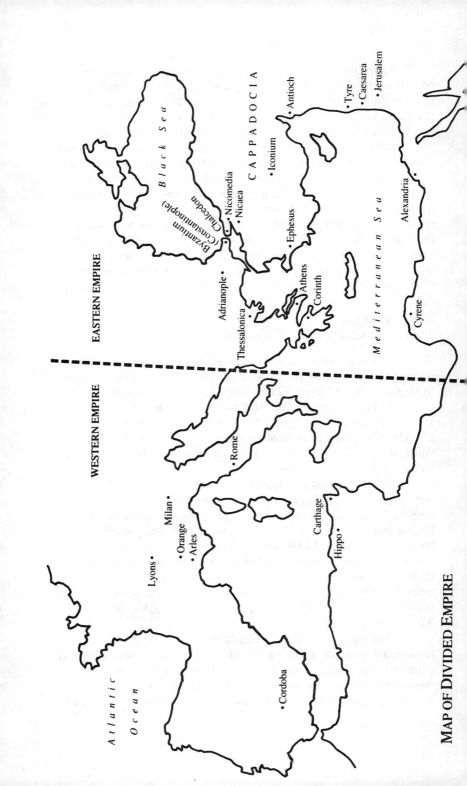

MAP OF DIVIDED EMPIRE

Eastern Church embraced the more abstract, the metaphysical. Thus we (Westerners) may find the chapters on the Western Church much more easily understandable than the chapters dealing with Eastern Christian thought.

If we are to understand and appreciate how the great Creeds developed, however, we are going to have to enter as best we can into the Eastern way of looking at things. That is because the theological debate underlying the great Creeds was carried out and resolved almost entirely in the East by Eastern Christians.

Perhaps the old saying, "Forewarned is forearmed," applies here. We should not suddenly think that there is something wrong with our mental processes once we reach the material in Chapters Four through Seven. In these chapters we Western pragmatists are on foreign soil. It will require a little time and attention for us to learn the different customs of our Eastern hosts.

Eastern Christians differed from Western Christians in much the same way as life in the ancient Greek city-state differed from life in the Rome of Christ's time. Even though there was a great deal of interaction between the two cultures, the Greek mind adapted itself more readily to abstract thought while the Roman mind was more practical in nature.

Western Christians were interested in how the theological debates affected liturgy, Church discipline, leadership and episcopal authority. They were little concerned with speculating for speculation's sake. The Eastern Christians, on the other hand, saw the practical implications of the theological debates, but they approached these debates more from their need to arrive at correct *theoretical* solutions which would safeguard truth and intellectual integrity.

In the pages ahead we will discuss this Eastern, theoretical approach first, *before* we fully develop the concerns of Western Christianity. This may strike our Western minds as "putting the cart before the horse." But I hope that in the end our "Eastern-first" approach will start to make more sense.

THOUGHT, BELIEF, EVENTS

In this book we will focus on the Church's attempt to synthesize faith and reason through the means of the great Creeds. Since the Creeds are products of both *thought* and *belief*, we can ignore neither the early Church's thinking nor its belief in piecing together the story behind the great Creeds. However, since the records of Christian *thinking* are more tangible than the records of Christian *belief*, we will of necessity tend to emphasize thought more than belief. This book, then, is more a history of early Christian thought than it is of early Christian belief.

We will find again and again, however, that it is often impossible to draw a line between what the early Christians thought about—their speculation about the gospel—and their innermost beliefs. In the pages ahead we may often find ourselves asking, "Which is more significant here, thought or belief?"

The intriguing aspect of the story behind the early Church is that we are in constant touch with this interplay between thought and belief, faith and reason. That is why we will concentrate on the Creeds as the focal point of early Church history: In the Creeds thinking and belief, reason and faith, merge and become one.

Our concern with thought and belief does not mean, however, that we can ignore a third key ingredient in early Church history. We could call this third ingredient *events*. Events are the one thing about history that everyone dreads: names, dates, places, battles, elections, etc. Who can remember all this minutiae? And, the reader of history usually asks, "Who cares?"

In the pages ahead we will try not to get lost in a forest of insignificant events. Yet, from chapter to chapter we will touch on the events and happenings surrounding the early Christian world.*

It is impossible to understand a history of Christian thought and belief without some background information. The early Church did not come into a world that was already Christian; it came into a world that had for centuries been developing its own social and political institutions as well as its own thought patterns and belief systems. Therefore, before we begin our discussion of early Christian thought and belief, let us situate the early Church in the world in which it found itself. In Chapter One we shall see how the Church lived out its life within that world down to about the year 312 A.D.

---

*Timelines to help keep the "events" in perspective can be found on page 20 (95 A.D. to 312 A.D.) and page 120 (312 A.D. to 600 A.D.). Unfamiliar terms can be found in the glossary.

CHAPTER ONE

THE CHURCH WITHOUT THE TWELVE

95 A.D.—312 A.D.: An Overview

What do we mean by "early Christianity?" The period under consideration in this book is 95 A.D. to about 600 A.D. Before 95 A.D. we are still in close touch with the "Age of Apostles"—those men whom Jesus personally selected and in and through whom Jesus founded his Church.

After 95 A.D. the Apostles are gone and their influence on the Church is exercised through newcomers on the Christian scene—people who had not known Jesus personally. One of the central questions of this post-apostolic Church was precisely how to continue apostolicity in the absence of the Apostles.

The end point of our inquiry—c. 600 A.D.—is chosen for three reasons. First of all, by this date the results of the great debates of early Church history have begun to be transformed into *norms* of medieval Christianity. Second, by the year 600 Western and Eastern Christianity have embarked on distinctly divergent paths. Finally, by the beginning of the seventh century the Christian faith is rooted firmly in the tradition not only of the New Testament writers and the teachings of the Apostles, but also in the writings of the great Christian thinkers ("the Fathers") of the post-apostolic era.

In this first chapter we want to look at key "events" during the first half of the early Church period, roughly 95 A.D. to 312 A.D. We will pick up the continuing story of "events" in Chapter Eight.

APOSTOLICITY WITHOUT APOSTLES

It is difficult for us to appreciate the predicament which confronted those Christians who first lived in a Church bereft of apostolic leadership. In the first days following Pentecost, Jesus' disciples had thought they were living in the "end times." They expected Jesus to come again very soon, certainly within the lifetime of the 12 Apostles. It wasn't long, however, before this expectation of an imminent Parousia began to wane.

There had never been any doubt that the Church was apostolic—that is, founded on and guided by the Apostles' transmission of Jesus' gospel. Bishop Clement of Rome about the year 95 states this clearly in a letter to the Church in Corinth:

> Now the Gospel was given to the Apostles for us by the Lord Jesus Christ....That is to say, Christ received his commission from God, and the Apostles theirs from Christ. The order of these two events was in accordance with the will of God.[1]

The problem for the post-apostolic Church was how to continue apostolicity without Apostles. Paul had written, "...God has set up in the church *first* apostles, *second* prophets, *third* teachers, then miracle workers, healers, assistants, administrators, and those who speak in tongues" (1 Corinthians 12:28; emphases added). Prophets, teachers, miracle workers and the rest could be replaced, but how did one replace an Apostle?

Bishops

The early Church found its answer in the person of the bishop. The first bishops were elders picked by the Apostles and commissioned by them to continue the work of the Twelve. According to Clement, as the Apostles "went through the territories and townships preaching, they appointed their first converts to be bishops and deacons for the believers of the future."[2] (In the context of Clement's letter it is clear that "bishops" were the successors of the Apostles, while "deacons" were the bishops' assistants.)

The early Christians thus believed that apostolicity continued on in the office of bishop. Ignatius, Bishop of Antioch, while being transported to Rome for execution about 105, reminded the Church at Tralles, "You should never act independently of your bishop—as evidently you do not."[3]

Like Clement, his fellow bishop in Rome, Ignatius also wrote of the bishops' assistants. Unlike Clement, however, who spoke only of deacons, Ignatius referred to bishop, deacon and *presbyter* (priest). "Without these three orders," Ignatius wrote, "no church has any right to the name."[4]

Priests

The development of the priesthood grew out of the office of bishop. And we may surmise that the early priesthood was at first more important in the Eastern Church. (Note above that, while Ignatius of Antioch counts priests as essential, Clement of Rome did not even mention this class of Church leaders.) This would be in keeping with what we otherwise know of the contrasting geographical developments of the Western and Eastern Churches.

The early Western Church was at first confined to cities. Since the first Christian communities in cities were small, one bishop sufficed to take care of the spiritual needs of the flock. In the East, however, there was a very early proliferation into rural areas. As small villages and rural hamlets gained converts, it became increasingly more difficult for one bishop to tend personally to his flock. The bishops thus ordained assistants to administer Baptism and officiate at the Eucharist. These assistants were the first Christian priests.

Deacons

The deacons, both in the West and the East, had as their responsibility administration of the local Church's practical affairs, particularly its finances. The bishop was first and foremost the spiritual father of his flock, *not* an administrator or clerical businessman. His assistant in the sacramental realm was the priest, and in the administrative realm the deacon. Of course, all three classes of elders intermingled certain duties when necessity dictated. Sometimes bishops administered, and priests and deacons preached and taught.

Everyday Spiritual Life

As is the case today, ordinary Christians in the early Church had to make a living, raise families and face the question of how to live their Christianity in a world opposed to the gospel. One huge difference between the early Christians and ourselves, however, lies in the degree of hostility expressed against the early Church by its contemporary society. Later in this chapter we will take a look at the most violent form of this hostility, the persecutions. But first, let's look briefly at the early

Church's everyday spiritual life.

Baptism: Entrance Into New Life

In the early Church, Baptism was the greatest of moments. Through this sacrament the early Christians expressed—and the Church publicly affirmed—their life-changing decision to accept Jesus Christ and his gospel. The early Church took this rite of initiation so seriously that it required a lengthy *catechumenate*, or period of instruction, for all who sought the sacrament.

The catechumenate varied in length and content from place to place. In Rome the catechumenate lasted three years and was carried out under very specific regulations, including regular supervision of the *catechumen* (person seeking Baptism) by a spiritual guide, the catechumen's performance of good works among the poor and needy, interrogation and prayers of exorcism by the bishop, study of the gospel and periodic fasting. When the early Christians finally reached the rite of Baptism itself, they knew what they were doing—that is, they *understood* their *faith*.

Baptism itself usually took place during the Easter vigil. Entire families were baptized together, each person stripping off his or her clothes (before either deacons or deaconesses, depending on one's sex) to enter the baptismal font. Here the bishop and his priests first poured the sacramental water over their heads and then anointed them with the oil of thanksgiving. After putting their clothes back on, the new Christians returned to the congregation and, for the first time, recited the Lord's Prayer with their new family of faith and partook of the Eucharist.

The early Church saw three effects in Baptism:

1) *Remission of sins.* According to Bishop Irenaeus of Lyons (c. 130-200), "As we are lepers in sin, we are made clean by means of sacred water and the invocation of the Lord from our old transgressions, being spiritually regenerated as newborn babes."[5]

2) *Salvation through Christ.* Clement of Alexandria (c. 150-215) described this effect of Baptism as an "illumination, perfection and washing: washing, by which we wash away our sins; grace, by which the penalties accruing to transgressions are remitted; and illumination, with which that holy light of salvation is beheld, that is, by which we see God clearly."[6]

3) *Gift of the Holy Spirit.* Bishop Cyprian of Carthage (d. 258) stressed, "Water alone is not able to cleanse away sins and to sanctify a man, unless he also has the Holy Spirit....There is no Baptism where the Holy Spirit is not, because there cannot be Baptism without the Spirit."[7]

Eucharist: The Body of Christ

From reading early Christian sources such as the *Didache* (pronounced Did-ah-kay) or *Teaching*, it is obvious that the Eucharist was a constituent element of early Church worship. But what did the early Christians *mean* by the Eucharist? Bishop Irenaeus of Lyons, claiming the authority of the Apostles' own teaching, wrote,

> For as the bread taken from the earth, when it has received the consecration from God, is no longer common bread but is the Eucharist, which consists of two realities, earthly and heavenly; so also our bodies, when they receive the Eucharist, are no longer corruptible, but have the hope of the resurrection unto eternal life.[8]

Did the early Church, then, understand the Eucharist to be the "real presence" of Christ? Let us again turn to the sources. Bishop Ignatius of Antioch, writing about 105, criticized certain heretics who "even absent themselves from the Eucharist and the public prayers, because they will not admit that the Eucharist is the self-same body of our savior Jesus Christ which suffered for our sins, and which the Father in his goodness afterwards raised up again."[9]

In another letter Ignatius called the Eucharist "the medicine of immortality, and the sovereign remedy by which we escape death and live in Jesus Christ for evermore."[10] Another Christian writer, Justin Martyr, writing perhaps 50 years after Ignatius, calls the Eucharist "the flesh and blood of that Jesus who was made flesh."[11]

These sources and others affirm that the early Church thought of the Eucharist as the real presence of Jesus Christ. To ask whether the early Church expressed this as "transubstantiation" or "consubstantiation" is an anachronistic question, one which early Christian minds would not have understood. The early Christians did not concern themselves with the *process* by which Jesus' presence became manifest in the Eucharist. Such questions became intriguing inquiries only for the minds of medieval Christians.

One thing is certain, however. The early Church believed it came to know Jesus "in the breaking of the bread" (Luke 24:35), and it placed the celebration of his presence in the Eucharist at the center of its worship.

As with Baptism, the early Church likewise developed a rite for the celebration of the Eucharist. Justin Martyr described this rite as it was celebrated in Rome about the year 150: Christians came together on "the day named after the sun," first to hear readings from "the memoirs of the Apostles and the writings of the prophets."[12] (Notice that at this early date Justin does not say "New Testament.") After a homily, the sacrificial gifts of bread and wine were brought forward to the priest, who stretched forth his hands over them and offered a prayer of consecration and thanksgiving. Then the members of the congregation passed around pieces of the bread given to them by the priest, and all drank from the common cup.

One striking thing in Justin's account is the degree to which the laity participated in the celebration. The early Eucharists were small affairs, usually celebrated around a table in someone's home. The ceremony was a social event as well as a religious act; celebrant and people communicated freely, and all were seen as full participants in the ritual.

Forgiveness of Sins

Nearly everyone in the earliest days thought it inconceivable that a Christian would renounce his or her Baptism by falling into serious sin. After all, being admitted to Baptism in the first place was no easy matter. (Murder, adultery and apostasy were generally held to be the chief "mortal" sins which served to renounce one's baptismal vows.) Thus, many took what for us may seem a very rigorous approach to post-baptismal sin.

The early Christians felt that once a person was baptized and sinned grievously, he or she should be offered only one opportunity for reconciliation with the Church. No second opportunity was offered, except perhaps on one's deathbed.

Because of this rigorist attitude many waited until a lengthy illness or old age to be baptized. Such people believed it only prudent to wait until the power of temptation was at a minimum before being baptized.

This type of thinking was hardly in keeping with the Church's understanding of Baptism as the sacrament of spiritual regeneration in which one received the Holy Spirit's power to resist sin. Such an attitude on the part of many believers, plus the growing realization that many Christians fell into sin again and again, prompted many bishops to reexamine the rigorist doctrine which offered only one chance for reconciliation.

Quite a debate began over this subject. The rigorist position was advanced by various Christian thinkers. One of the earliest was a writer named Hermas who, about the year 150, expressed the prevalent view:

After that great and holy calling, if anyone sins who has been tempted by the devil, he has one repentance. But if he continually sins and repents, it is of no advantage to such a man, for he will hardly live. [13]

A stormy controversy over this question began to develop during the tenure of the Roman Bishop Callistus (217-222). Callistus was a pragmatist who felt that the Church should accommodate the good and the bad, the "wheat and the tares" (cf. Matthew 13:30, one of the bishop's favorite Scripture passages). Thus he ordained as priests men with dubious reputations.

A scholarly Roman priest named Hippolytus (170-236) was upset by what he saw as Callistus' moral laxity, which he thought had infected the entire Church. Hippolytus wrote a very idealistic work called *Church Order*, by which he hoped to return the Church to the (as he saw it) pristine purity of apostolic times.

The Western bishops gradually came to reject Hippolytus's views on reconciliation, and the rigorist position began to dissolve. In its place developed a ritual of penance by which recurring sinners could be reconciled.

This more lenient view of penance had already existed in the East as early as about 220. The *Didascalia*, a Syrian work of about that date, gives a detailed picture of the Eastern Church's requirements for post-baptismal penance.

According to the *Didascalia* it is the bishop's duty to correct sinners in his flock by excluding them temporarily from communion with the Church. Once the congregation finds the sinner's repentance to be sincere, the full body of believers (led by the deacons) approaches the bishop to ask for reconciliation for their sinful brother or sister.

The bishop then imposes a suitable penance (usually involving fasting). The penance phase lasts until the bishop and the entire community is assured of the sinner's firmness of purpose not to sin again. (Note that penance was an entirely *public* affair.) Then, in the presence of the entire congregation, the bishop imposes hands and readmits the sinner to full communion with the body. The interesting point is that the Didascalia nowhere suggests that this process could take place only once.

The above account of everyday spiritual life may suggest that Christian life from 95-312 was placid, calm and concerned only with "spiritual" matters. Such was hardly the case. Because of the Roman Empire's hostility to this subversive new movement, the early Christians often found their everyday lives chaotic and imperiled by great dangers to both person and property.

THE CHURCH PERSECUTED

The history of Christian persecutions is linked to the history of the Empire itself. As that latter history is a very complex one, so too is the history of the Church persecuted.

First of all, the years from Emperor Domitian's death in 96 until Emperor Constantine's rise to power in 312 were not years of constant persecution. There were periods of benign neglect under some emperors, and even brief periods of toleration.

Secondly, not all emperors gave as much attention to Christianity (and thus to its persecution) as other emperors did. Remember that the Roman political situation was precarious during the centuries of the Church's persecution. Several emperors worried less about the spread of Christianity than about preserving the Empire's crumbling institutions and diminishing frontiers.

Thirdly, not all places in the Christian world experienced persecution to the same degree of harshness. In some parts of the Empire (generally speaking, the Western half), the Church was less threatened than in other regions. As the Empire's center of gravity shifted from Rome to Byzantium (its new Eastern capital), the Empire concentrated its efforts to exterminate the Church in the Eastern regions where, incidentally, the Christian population was greater.

Finally, we must dispel the old myth of every Christian marching bravely to death rather than accepting pagan religion. The truth of the matter is that, in places and times where persecution was most vicious, the *majority* of Christians apostatized in one form or another.

Yet it is also true that in times and places of the utmost cruelty there arose a Christian minority of the utmost valor. The testimony of these witnesses to the faith—these martyrs (from the Greek word for "witness")—far overshadowed the weakness of others who denied their faith.

With these qualifications in mind, let us now sketch a brief outline of the Empire's relationship to Christianity from 95 to 312. Since our principal objective is to show how the events of these years affected what Christians thought and what they believed, we will compress many details into a highly generalized picture. (The chart on pp. 20-21 might help you to keep these details straight.)

Illegal to 'Be' a Christian

Emperor Trajan (98-117) established the legal principle that one could be punished simply for *being* a Christian. No proof of other violation of the established criminal code was necessary to condemn a Christian to death. Yet Trajan did not decree that Christians were to be vigorously hunted down as criminals. Only if several witnesses came forward with proof of offensive conduct (such as refusing to worship the emperor) would the authorities proceed against alleged Christians. In some areas Trajan's decision turned out to be a blessing in disguise for the

Church; Roman governors were not *required* to institute persecutions if they chose not to do so.

Nonetheless, the *Acts of the Martyrs* (writings depicting the martyrs' deaths) demonstrate that Trajan's policy certainly did not guarantee the Church peace and security. Simeon, the second Bishop of Jerusalem (after James, the brother of the Lord), was crucified during Trajan's rule. And the most famous martyr of the early Church, Bishop Ignatius of Antioch, was transported during Trajan's reign from Antioch to Rome for a hideous execution. About the year 107 Ignatius was led into the Colosseum before a packed audience who watched gleefully as wild animals tore him to pieces.

Emperor Hadrian (117-138) continued Trajan's policy of not seeking out Christians for prosecution. Nonetheless, it remained a crime under Hadrian for one merely to be a Christian.

Under Emperor Antoninus (138-161) another famous martyr, Bishop Polycarp of Smyrna, lost his life for the faith. According to the contemporary account which has come down to us, a Roman governor demanded of Polycarp, "Take the oath [to Caesar] and I will let you go....Revile your Christ." Polycarp replied, "Eighty-six years have I served him, and he has done me no wrong. How then can I blaspheme my king and my savior?"[14] Before the hysterical crowd Polycarp was then burned alive. The writer of the account states that Polycarp "was the 12th to meet a martyr's death in Smyrna."[15] Since Polycarp died about the year 155, we can conclude that the earliest persecutions—though intense in the hatred shown for Christians—had not struck down a great number of the faithful.

A 'Deadly' Policy Change

When Emperor Septimius Severus (193-211) came to the imperial throne he began a deadly change in Rome's policy toward the Church. Severus realized that Trajan's policy had been ineffectual in restricting the growth of the new faith. In 202, therefore, Severus issued an edict making it illegal for people to *convert* to Christianity, and he put his army and police to work to enforce this edict. The emperor's policy was aimed at the young Church's successful missionary activities. Severus wanted to eliminate the spread of Christianity by making it politically and socially detrimental for one to accept the Christian faith.

Emperor Decius (249-251) went Severus one step better. In 250 he required everyone within the borders of the Empire to sacrifice to the Roman gods. Those who complied with this edict were given a certificate, or *libellus*. Anyone who could not present the authorities with a *libellus* upon demand was imprisoned, tortured and, upon final refusal to sacrifice, executed.

Decius' persecution constituted a serious threat to the life of the young Church. Along with those Christians who actually sacrificed to the gods (*sacrificati*), others (nicknamed *libellatici*) bribed Roman officials to sell them a *libellus*. Still others paid imposters to go to the authorities and present a *libellus* under an assumed Christian name. The general name for those who capitulated to Decius' edict was *lapsi* (the lapsed ones).

The ranks of the *lapsi* included bishops, one of whom even persuaded his own flock to offer sacrifice to the Roman gods. As in earlier persecutions, however, there were everywhere those who held fast to the faith. Once Decius' persecution passed, the accounts of martyrdom began to surface. Bishop Dionysius of Alexandria, for example, wrote of many witnesses for the faith in Egypt. Bishop Alexander of Jerusalem and Bishop Babylas of Antioch had themselves been put to death by Decius' agents.

Emperor Valerian (253-260) continued Decius' brutal repression of the Church. During Valerian's persecution one of the early Church's greatest thinkers lost his life. Cyprian of Carthage was a pagan intellectual who converted to Christianity in 246. Elected bishop by the people of Carthage in 248, he was unquestionably the greatest bishop of the Western Church until his death in 258.

Cyprian had fled from Carthage during Decius' reign, shepherding his flock from exile. Upon his return in 251 he was faced with the problem of the *lapsi*. Cyprian's thinking on this issue influenced the theology of Christian North Africa until the seventh century.

Cyprian believed that lay persons among the *lapsi* should be readmitted to the Church only after performing penance. In the case of the *sacrificati* (those who actually sacrificed to the gods), such penance was to last an entire lifetime; reconciliation with the Church could take place only on one's deathbed. Clergy among the *lapsi* should be *permanently* excommunicated. As we shall see in Chapter Four, Cyprian's rigorist viewpoint was to have great influence on the Donatist controversy of the fourth and fifth centuries.

After Cyprian's death, Emperor Valerian's son Gallienus (260-268), besieged by troubles on every side, decided to make peace with the Christians. He did this in remarkable fashion. With his edict of 260, Emperor Gallienus began a series of measures which granted the Church an unprecedented degree of imperial protection and support. The emperor restored confiscated Church properties, allowed Christians freedom of belief and worship, permitted them to make converts and brought many Christians into high office in his own government.

Gallienus's policy of toleration outlived him by 30 years. During the period 260-300 the Church—though not a legally sanctioned religion—enjoyed an uninterrupted (if uneasy) peace. Soon, however, the Christian dream of a new era of harmony between Church and State turned into a nightmare.

The 'Final Solution'

During the first two decades of his rule, Emperor Diocletian (284-305) adhered to Gallienus's policy of toleration. Beginning about 300, however, Diocletian did an abrupt about-face and instituted the last and most savage of all the persecutions of the Christian Church (called "the Great Persecution").

In 303, in the Eastern portion of the Empire where Diocletian had his capital, persecution broke loose like a wild animal suddenly unleashed. Churches were destroyed; Bibles, hymnals, psalters and other sacred writings were burned; celebration of the Mass and all other acts of worship were forbidden. Christians in government posts were subjected to the cruelest of tortures. Church leaders were arrested in great numbers.

According to the contemporary Church historian, Eusebius (c. 260-340), there were so many bishops, priests and deacons in jail that ordinary criminals had no place to be incarcerated. As in previous persecutions, sacrifice to the Roman gods was required of all.

In contrast to the dreadful situation in the East, the co-emperor in the West, Maximian (and Maximian's second-in-command—a highly respected old general named Constantius), refused to adhere closely to Diocletian's terrorist policies. Church property was confiscated here and there, but no one was killed or imprisoned. Eastern Christians, on the other hand, withstood the harshest of attacks for a full eight years.

When both Maximian in the West and Diocletian in the East abdicated in 305, Constantius became emperor in the West and a man named Galerius became co-emperor in the East. The persecution in the East was finally lifted in 311 when Galerius issued an edict of toleration. Surpassing the policy of Gallienus a half-century earlier, Galerius allowed Christianity to be practiced as freely and openly as any other religion. In the West Constantius welcomed Galerius's official change of policy. Constantius's tolerant attitude was shared by his son Constantine, who in 306 succeeded his father as emperor in the West.

CONSTANTINE, CHRISTIAN EMPEROR

Having survived the final and most vicious assault by the Roman Empire, the Church did not require an emperor's conversion to assure its

17

continued growth. Severus, Decius, Valerian and Diocletian, through the most barbarous of persecutions, had been unable to eliminate Christianity because the Church had become an inevitable movement within the Empire. Galerius's edict of 311 was, therefore, not so much a peace treaty with Christianity as an instrument of surrender. The Empire realized that the Church was there to stay; Roman power had been unable to stop its progress.

This raises the question of the significance of Constantine's conversion to Christianity. Was Constantine's conversion really a conversion (that is, a radical turning away from his previous way of life in favor of the gospel) or merely the acknowledgment of a *fait accompli*? Did Constantine consciously choose a new form of religious existence for himself and for the Empire, or did he merely jump with the Empire onto the bandwagon of an inexorable movement—a movement which everywhere was replacing the ancient Roman institutions? The answer—like Constantine's personality itself—is not easily known.

Constantine's father, as we have seen, was only a halfhearted persecutor of the Church. There is evidence that one and perhaps two of Constantine's sisters were Christians even during Diocletian's reign. Constantine's family thus appears to have been well-disposed toward Christianity even before Constantine became co-emperor of the West in 306. There is no doubt that Constantine's early upbringing had been strongly influenced by monotheism. As a result Constantine sought for a way to link his political fortunes to the power of the one omnipotent God.

By Constantine's time the Empire had become more and more unmanageable. Thus, as already indicated, two coequal centers of administration had been set up, one in the East and one in the West. The Eastern capital was established first in Nicomedia and then in Byzantium (later renamed Constantinople), and the Western capital remained in Rome. The two co-emperors, or *augusti*, each had an assistant, or *caesar*. Needless to say, each *augustus* wanted to dominate the other and to return the Empire to united leadership. In addition, Constantine's *caesar* in the West, Maxentius, sought to overthrow Constantine as Western *augustus*. But at the Battle of the Milvian Bridge in 312, Constantine soundly defeated his rival and became undisputed ruler in the West.

The night before this battle Constantine is said to have had a dream in which God instructed him to inscribe on his soldiers' shields a symbol for the name of Christ—the letter X turned sideways with the top arm bent over, later called the *labarum*. Constantine heeded the words of the dream, and the next day led his troops into battle under the patronage of the Christian God. The historian Eusebius adds that before the battle

Constantine saw the *labarum* revealed in the sky beside the words, "By this, conquer."

Whether this story is factual or legendary, the important point is that from 312 on Constantine gradually came to see himself as chosen by the Christian God to promote Christianity and to unite the fortunes of the Empire with those of the Church. Constantine did not make Christianity the "official" Roman religion; rather, he gradually made it the *favored* religion. But in the Roman mind the two concepts became virtually synonymous. It was now obvious in which direction the religious future of the Empire lay, and many former enemies of the Church abruptly "converted" to the previously despised "superstition."

Constantine was not another St. Paul, nor did his conversion constitute a dramatic, life-changing acceptance of Jesus as Lord and Savior. Constantine was a pagan through and through, and it took years for his pagan mind to grasp the full implications of the Christian gospel. He did not ask to be baptized until shortly before his death in 337—some 25 years after his conversion. During those years, however, there is no doubt that Constantine gradually became a sincere Christian.

Constantine, who saw himself as protected by the banner of Christ, eventually realized his dream of bringing the Empire under his sole rule. In 324 he defeated the *augustus* of the East, Licinius, and become sole *augustus* of a reunited Empire. From this time on, in one document after another, Constantine reveals his conviction that the Christian God had chosen him "to spread the most blessed faith."

Of his new divine patron Constantine writes, "I owe him my whole soul, every breath and every stirring of my mind wholly and completely." He equates Christianity with the "divine law," and he promises God to "follow the same dispositions of your power and to battle against your enemies. For that I have consecrated my soul to you."[16]

With Constantine's conversion we conclude this "background" chapter on the events of the first half of early Church history. We now begin the major thrust of this book, the dialogue between faith and reason and the development of the great Creeds.

TIMELINE: 95 A.D.—312 A.D.

Emperors

Domitian (81-96)

Trajan (98-117)

Ignatius of Antioch martyred (107)

Hadrian (117-138)

Antoninus (138-161)

Polycarp of Smyrna martyred (c. 155)

Septimius Severus (193-211)

Irenaeus of Lyons (200)

Bishops of Rome (Popes)

Clement (88-96)

Pius I (140-155)

Victor (189-198)

Zephyrinus (199-217)

---

c.95: End of the Age of the Apostles

100

Trajan makes it illegal to be a Christian

105: Ignatius of Antioch coins term "Catholic Church"

c.140: Ancient Roman symbol (R) in use; prototype of later Creeds

140: Marcion founds his rival Church

144: Marcion is excommunicated

150: Hermas advances the rigorist position on forgiveness of post-baptismal sin

Gnostic Valentinus gains a following

Writings of Justin Martyr (265), first classically educated apologist

c.170: Athenagoras writes on Trinity

c.178: Celsus' True Discourse (an anti-Christian polemic)

200

202: Becomes illegal to *convert* to Christianity

Sabellius promotes Modalist views in Rome

Callistus (217-222)

Clement of Alexandria (c.215)

Tertullian (225)

Hippolytus (c.236)

Stephen (254-257)

c.220: *Didascalia* describes non-rigorist view toward post-baptismal penance

250: Everyone required to sacrifice to Roman gods
Cyprian of Carthage and Stephen of Rome debate validity of sacramental ministers
260: Gallienus's policy of toleration inaugurates 40-year era of peace
Term *homoousios* first introduced

286: Empire divided into East and West

300: "The Great Persecution"
c.306: Synod of Elvira requires continence of all married clergy
Miltiades (311-314)
311: Galerius issues an edict of toleration
312: Battle of Milvian Bridge and Constantine's conversion; Christianity becomes "favored" religion
313: Constantine supports Synod of Arles and represses Donatists

324: Constantine becomes sole ruler of reunited Empire

300

Decius (249-251)
Valerian (253-260)   Origen (c.254)
Gallienus (260-268) Dionysius of Alexandria (264)
Dionysius of Rome (268)

Diocletian (284-305) in East
and Maximian (286-305) in West

Constantius (305-306) in West
and Galerius (305-311) in East

Constantine (306-324) in West
and Licinius (311-324) in East

Single dates in parentheses indicate an
individual's date of death; dates spanning a
number of years refer to time in office.

CHAPTER TWO

'WE TELL NO INCREDIBLE TALES'

The Gospel Confronts Pagan Philosophy

Christianity was at first entirely a Jewish phenomenon. Its first evangelists and writers were either Jews themselves or people thoroughly familiar with the Jewish way of thinking.

The pagan world had nothing to compare with the Jewish concept of God as *one*, *personal*, *transcendent* and *universal*. Pagan conceptions of God may have included one or more of these four elements, but not all of them at once. For example, pagans were familiar with personal deities—such as Zeus, the king of the Greek gods—but these deities' powers were never thought to extend throughout the entire world and over all peoples.

Some pagans, like Jews and Jewish Christians, did understand God to be both absolute and transcendent. These pagans, however, could not conceive of the absolute deity as a person in the sense that Yahweh was a person—that is, a God who had will, intelligence and the capacity for love. For pagans, the absolute was an "it" and not a "who."

In addition to these differing conceptions of God, pagans approached questions about God, truth and life very differently than the Jews. As was mentioned in the Introduction, pagans approached these issues from the point of view of *speculative philosophy*. The Jews (and the first Christians), on the other hand, had no philosophy. For them, knowledge of reality was a matter of *Yahweh's revelation* as seen through Yahweh's action in Israel's history. Thus Judeo-Christian thinkers were first and foremost *religious*; pagan intellectuals were first and foremost *philosophical*. The Jews and the first Jewish Christians had little room for speculation within their religious system. For the pagan philosophers, however, religious questions were merely a branch of an entire system of speculation.

When these two styles of thought—the revelatory and the speculative—confronted each other in Christianity, it produced quite a clash. Pagan intellectuals by and large looked upon Christianity as a crude, irrational Jewish cult that was unworthy of esteem by educated persons. They particularly despised the Christians' claim that Christ was the God of *all* peoples and that only through Christ was the salvation of humanity possible.

In that respect the pagan world was much like ours today: People thought it boorish for someone to claim the possession of absolute truth. The pagans prided themselves on their *syncretistic* mentality—that is, that they could find a little bit of truth in every proposition. It gravely offended them to hear Christians claim to possess the highest truth as revealed by God in the person of—not a great philosopher or thinker—but a humble Galilean woodworker who died an embarrassing and humiliating death.

Yet, as increasing numbers of non-Jews converted to Christianity, the Church began to recognize the need for formulating a response to the criticisms of pagan intellectuals. It did this by using the pagans' own thought systems to demonstrate the *intellectual* superiority of the Christian gospel. The religion of revelation thus entered into the world of speculative thought, and the consequences for both Christianity and pagan philosophy were literally world-changing.

Some see this confrontation between the gospel and philosophy as the downfall of the gospel's simple message of salvation. Why, such persons ask, did the Church think it necessary to muddy the waters of the original gospel revelation by getting involved in perverse intellectual speculation?

The answer, then as now, is human nature. People are comprised of intellect as well as will; and along with the will's desire to believe there is the intellect's quest to understand. It was to satisfy this natural human desire to *understand* the Christian revelation that the Church confronted pagan philosophy. The Church entered into dialogue with the pagan world in terms of that world's own systems of thought. Like St. Paul, the Church made itself "…all things to all men in order to save at least some of them" (1 Corinthians 9:22a).

SYSTEMS OF ANCIENT PHILOSOPHY

We cannot understand the Church's dialogue with philosophy unless we understand something about ancient philosophy itself. There were many systems of ancient philosophy and we cannot hope to consider all of them. We will discuss only the two most important systems for our study—Stoicism and Platonism—and focus on just three ideas: (1) God, (2) world and (3) the relationship between God and world.

Stoicism

Stoicism's underlying principle was this: Inherent in the universe is a "natural law" regulating and ordering all persons and events. Humanity in harmony with this natural law is peaceful and happy, while humanity in conflict with it is contentious and miserable. The goal of the Stoics, then, was to know the natural law and live it.

Although Stoicism began in Greece, it became the favorite philosophy of Roman imperial society during the early days of the Church. A Stoic philosopher named Seneca (4 B.C.-65 A.D.) tutored the young Nero and exercised great influence on affairs of state until the paranoid emperor forced Seneca to commit suicide.

Seneca developed two ethical ideas which greatly influenced Roman society during the early Christian era: (1) *inward self-control* in the face of all circumstances (whether outwardly "good" or "bad"—the Stoics believed value judgments were impossible) and (2) *submission of one's own interest* to the good of all humanity. Such a philosophy was obviously very useful to a totalitarian dictatorship like the Roman Empire, and could be manipulated to justify the most egregious of cruelties. By today's standards, nonetheless, most Stoics were highly moral people.

The Stoics were also *practical* people. They did not care as much about how or why things worked as about getting in tune with things as they actually did work. Yet, although most Stoics did not specialize in speculation for its own sake, they did produce a well-thought-out system to explain the world and its ways.

For Stoics God was an integrative force *within* the world which held the world together and directed its operation. God was a rational spirit which produced material creation and subsisted *in* this creation. God was not separate from the world; he was the vital soul *of* the world. All of creation—humanity included—was but the visible manifestation of God's activity. The Stoics were thus *monists*—that is, they thought everything was part of one and the same ultimate substance: God.

The ultimate goal within Stoicism was for the individual to

25

become godlike, which meant to become entirely in touch with God's—and thus the world's—order and harmony. To attain godlikeness the Stoics practiced the virtues of intelligence, justice, bravery and, especially, self-control. The result of practicing these virtues was a state of *apatheia*, a sort of inner tranquillity and peace which characterized a life in harmony with natural law, or God's own benevolent order. Oddly enough, much of Stoicism sounds a lot like parts of the Christian teaching. Look, for example, at Paul's writing in Galatians 5:22 and Romans 12:5.

For the Stoics the motivating force behind creation was the *logos*. This *logos*, which they defined as God the creator, was the actual "stuff" of God existing inside all matter. Like a drop of vinegar dispersed in a glass of water, the *logos* interpenetrated everything that was, including the human soul. The way to obtain harmony with nature (and thus God) was to become attuned to this inner *logos*.

When the writer of the Gospel of John used the same word, *logos*, to refer to the eternal Word of God (John 1:1), he was obviously trying to present the message of God's revelation in a way that would appeal to non-Jews such as the Stoics. The Gospel writer, of course, meant something much different. For the Stoics the *logos* was one with and inseparable from the world. For John the *logos* was the transcendent God who fully became man in a world that was *distinct* from God.

Platonism

Plato was unquestionably the most influential philosopher of the early Church period even though he died 350 years before Jesus' birth. While Plato's original thought had undergone certain modifications by the New Testament era, the stamp of his thinking was nonetheless clearly impressed on nearly every philosophical system then in vogue.

The core of Plato's philosophy is his "theory of forms." Plato taught that material creation is ever-changing and thus incapable of being truly known. Yet Plato perceived an unchanging "something" underlying all changing reality.

Take, for example, chairs: No matter how many different chairs there are in the world, Plato thought, all chairs participate in the one universal quality called "chair-ness." This is the unchanging, absolute reality which underlies all individual chairs. This "chair-ness" was not just a concept, Plato said, but an actual reality, or *form*, which exists in and of itself. Therefore, even if all the individual chairs which one can actually see and touch were destroyed, the *form* of "chairness" would still exist.

For Plato such forms were the only objects of true knowledge.

One could know truth only by perceiving the unchanging forms underlying changing events, things and persons. A philosopher is a person who seeks out knowledge of the forms. To attain such knowledge is to be in touch with ultimate reality.

How does one come to an awareness of forms? Through the soul, the one element of the human person which is unchanging and absolute. For Plato, then, the individual soul is eternal; it *preexists* the individual person who eventually takes on a material appearance. Notice how different this is from Christian revelation, which says that God creates each person's soul out of nothing when each person comes into existence.

What was the highest form (the form of forms, so to speak) or the final reality greater than which none existed? Plato pointed to the ultimate form which he called the GOOD. The GOOD came very close for Plato to being God, although he distinguished in his writings between the two.

Contrary to the Stoics who were monists ("all is one"), Plato was a *dualist*: He believed God and the world to be separate. God was the absolute and ultimate transcendent reality, above and beyond the world of the senses. Notice how similar this is to the Jewish concept of Yahweh as the absolute, transcendent God, above and beyond all material creation.

In order to "arrange" the world (Plato did not believe in creation from nothing) and to sustain it, God employs a "craftsman" known as the demiurge. (See how the Jews used this concept of God's "craftsman" in Proverbs 8:22-31.)

Plato's demiurge attempts to pattern material things after the various eternal forms. The first things which the demiurge molds are lesser gods, then the world's soul and, finally, the human soul and body. Notice that none of these things are brought into being by the demiurge; they are simply shaped from a preexisting form into a state of order and cohesion.

Plato developed a view of the world as *graded* in godlikeness from the supreme God to the lowest particle of physical creation. The farther one moved away from God in this graded order, the less in touch with the ultimate reality one was. A great distinction is therefore made in Platonism between the more godlike "spiritual" world and the less godlike "material" world.

As we shall see in the next chapter, the Gnostic heretics of the early Church hyper-extended Plato's dichotomy between spirit and matter. In their dualistic world, matter was seen as evil and spirit as good. In this perversion of Plato's thought, the demiurge became the dark lord who, either carelessly or for evil motives, created both the foul earth and despicable human beings.

Not just heretics, however, had trouble with this dichotomy between spirit and matter. Plato's dualism greatly affected orthodox Christian thinkers as well. Many orthodox Christians also wondered if perhaps "spirit" was not of more value than "flesh." This question was at the core of later controversies over the meaning of the incarnation. By becoming man, had God truly ennobled flesh? Or had God in effect only "pretended" to tolerate human flesh long enough to save it?

One Platonist who addressed this spirit-flesh dichotomy was Plutarch (45-125). He developed what came to be the generally held Platonic concept of God during the early Church era. Notice how Plutarch strives to describe God in terms that are utterly pure and transcendent, far removed from the vain pursuits of earthly mortals:

> While we are here below, encumbered by bodily affections, we can have no intercourse with God save as in philosophic thought we may faintly touch him, as in a dream. But when our souls are released, and have passed into the region of the pure, invisible and changeless, this God will be the guide and king of those who depend on him and gaze with insatiable longing on the beauty which may not be spoken of by the lips of man.[1]

This emphasis on God's utter transcendence was likewise stressed by a prolific anti-Christian Platonist named Celsus (second century). Celsus denied that God had any contact with material creation whatsoever—and especially not with human beings. God sullied his hands with mortals only through the use of demons. How crude such pagan philosophers must have found Christian beliefs such as, "the Word became *flesh* and made his dwelling among us" (John 1:14, emphasis added).

About the mid-third century Platonism took on a different cast through the writings of a man named Plotinus. Plotinus's major achievement was to define God in terms of three *hypostases* or natures. Plotinus called these "The One," "Intellect" and "Soul." *The One* is the ultimate and transcendent absolute, beyond being itself. Everything in the world comes from The One by a process called *emanation* (not creation), and seeks a return to The One.

Then, through *Intellect,* The One brings the rest of creation into existence. By contemplating The One, the Intellect produces *Soul,* which is the underlying principle of human beings. The farther one moves from The One, that is, the more one moves away from spirit and in the direction of matter, the more one moves from good to evil.

Plotinus thought matter was the source of evil. For Plotinus the moral life consisted in escaping the confines of matter and contemplating the higher realm of Intellect in hopes of one day merging back into The One.

Notice how such a concept could have struck some Christians as similar to the idea of dying and going to heaven to be "with God." Conversely many pagans, upon first hearing about the Christian idea of heaven, may have thought Christians were saying the same thing as Plotinus and other Platonists.

POINTS OF CONTACT WITH CHRISTIANITY

From the above outline it is obvious how many points of contact existed between Christianity and the ancient philosophies of Stoicism and Platonism.

The Stoics were on the whole very moral people. Their ethical system on its surface appeared quite compatible with many of St. Paul's moral exhortations. And the Stoic concepts of God's all-pervading universality and the corresponding universality of human relationships were very similar to Paul's thought: "The body is one and has many members, but all the members, many though they are, are one body; and so it is with Christ. It was in one Spirit that all of us, whether Jew or Greek, slave or free, were baptized into one body" (1 Corinthians 12:12-13a).

Further, many Christian thinkers elaborated upon John's use of the word *logos* to identify Christ as "Word" of the Father. In the process they gave Stoicism a markedly Christian demeanor (and Christianity something of a Stoic facade).

Just as Stoicism had points of contact with Christianity, so too Platonism was unquestionably compatible with Christianity's most basic religious principle—that God was one and transcendent, the final and ultimate power beyond all creation, immutable and eternal.

Plato's philosophy started to appear even more compatible with Judeo-Christian theology when a Jewish Platonist—Philo of Alexandria (d. 40 A.D.)—tried to harmonize Platonism and the Jewish revelation. Philo said, for example, that Yahweh in creating the world used as patterns the forms as they eternally existed in his mind.

And, with Plotinus's concept of The One, Intellect and Soul, we see obvious parallels to the Christian Trinity. To some Christian thinkers The One could very easily be translated into the Father, the Intellect into Son, and the Soul into Spirit.

Yet *compatibility* with pagan thought was not the same thing as *identity*. Christian thinkers saw the points of contact, but they also saw essential points of contrast. It was the task of the Christian "apologists" in explaining the gospel to pagan intellectuals both to affirm the value of the best pagan traditions and at the same time prove to the pagans how these traditions were fulfilled and superseded by the superior message of the Christian gospel.

CHRISTIAN APOLOGETICS

The word *apology* here means a formal defense and justification of one's beliefs. The Christian apologists were people who defended and justified Christianity for pagan thinkers.

The motive of the first apologists was uniquely practical. They sought to prevent the destruction of the Church by a Roman government which was entirely sympathetic to the attacks of pagan intellectuals. As we shall see, the apologists at first wrote in Greek, even in the West. Gradually, however, Western apologists began to write in Latin and to focus on more practical themes. The Eastern apologists—true to form—concentrated on abstract, conceptual issues.

Justin Martyr

The first true philosopher among the early Western apologists, and the first Christian thinker who could match the pagans' intellectual abilities, was Justin Martyr. Between his conversion in 130 and his death in 165, Justin's goal was to establish Christianity as "the only certain and adequate philosophy."[2] He sought to win over pagan intellectuals by praising their greatest ancestors—such as Socrates—for having known Christ in their own times through the working of the *logos* within their hearts.

Justin gave to the *logos* both the Stoic connotation of the rational spirit underlying all creation and the New Testament connotation of the preexistent Christ. Although they had not known it, Justin said, sincere pagan philosophers who dedicated their lives to the pursuit of truth had been guided all along by God's revelation in and through the *logos*. This revelation was a partial one, however, completed and fulfilled only with the actual manifestation of the *logos* in the person of Christ. Since the *logos* (which formerly operated through principles of natural law) has now become flesh, Justin asserted, full knowledge of truth depends upon knowledge of the logos-Christ, revealed historically in the person of Jesus.

Justin sought to justify Christianity in terms compatible with pagan thought, but he did not whitewash clear differences between pagan thought and the gospel.

In contrast to Plato's preexistent soul, Justin stressed the

Christian view: that the soul is not preexistent, but created out of nothing by God. In contrast to Platonists like Plutarch, he insisted that the goal of individual Christian life—resurrection from the dead—is not an "escape" from one's individual existence and collapse into the great all, but rather the fulfillment of one's personhood in a glorified body.

Justin was essentially a Christian Platonist. He stressed God's absoluteness and transcendence and, as a result, seemed to feel uncomfortable with the suggestion that the transcendent Father really entered into the affairs of humanity. Rather, Justin said, the Father's actions in history as recorded in the Old Testament should be thought of as manifestations of the *logos*.

Justin came very close to writing of the Christian *logos* as if it were one of the intermediary gods of Platonism. Justin never used the word *intermediary*, but he does call the incarnate Word "another God."[3] By this he meant that Christ is a "power" of God, just as the light from the sun is of the same nature as the sun itself, yet distinct from the sun.[4]

Justin's difficulty in describing the relationship between the absolute God and his *logos*, or the relationship between Father and Son, was but the first in a long series of difficulties to occupy Christian thinkers down to the end of our period of inquiry. Justin's effort to preserve the Christian revelation that "the Word was God" (John 1:1) while at the same time trying to satisfy the Platonic belief in God as transcendent and distinct from the world is the starting point of the great debate over the incarnation which will occupy us in the pages ahead.

Athenagoras

Another apologist, Athenagoras, addressed himself to Justin's dilemma. Athenagoras was the most lucid writer among the apologists. We are struck at such an early date (c. 170) by the astonishing accuracy of Athenagoras's understanding of the three persons in one God:

> ...[The Son] is the first product of the Father, not as having been brought into existence...but inasmuch as he came to be the idea and energizing power of all material things....The Holy Spirit himself also, which operates in the prophets, we assert to be an effluence of God, flowing from him, and returning back again like a beam of the sun.[5]

Tertullian

Justin and Athenagoras, as well as other Western apologists, wrote in Greek (the language used by the educated classes throughout the Empire). The first Western apologists to write in Latin were Minucius Felix and Tertullian (160-225), both lawyers and North Africans. They represented the more practical kind of apologetics which characterize the

Latin West. Both writers played a significant role in the development of Christian Latin. Until their time the Church (even in Rome) had preached, worshiped and written largely in Greek.

Tertullian is by far the more significant of the two men. Minucius wrote only one work, while Tertullian wrote at least 26 major treatises covering nearly every area of Christian life from *On the Soul* to *On the Dress of Women*. A complex figure, Tertullian started out as a staunch defender of episcopal authority and ended up as an advocate of personal prophecy and direct divine revelation—thus removing himself from the teaching of the Catholic Church.

His major work, *Apology*, is styled as a lawyer's plea for justice from the pagans. Unlike the more speculative Greek apologists, Tertullian is eminently practical. He asks the pagans to consider the illogic and injustice of their attack, based as it is on an ignorance of the true nature of Christianity. He then establishes the proper procedure by which the debate is to be conducted.

Tertullian's practical approach is illustrated by his attitude toward speculative philosophy. In *Prescription Against Heretics*, he wrote, "What has Athens to do with Jerusalem? What concord is there between the Academy and the Church?"[6] For Tertullian the key to belief was one's acceptance of divine revelation, not one's assent to speculative theories.

Tertullian's immense influence on the future development of Latin Christianity cannot even begin to be discussed in the space provided here. We will focus on just one aspect of his thought which, for our purposes, was to have the most far-reaching of consequences: Tertullian gave the Western Church a formula for understanding the Trinity that would be used for centuries. Tertullian's clarity of expression in *Against Praxeas* was to save the Western Church from the intense and often chaotic search for proper Trinitarian terminology which characterized theological speculation in the East.

To clarify the relationship of the three divine persons, Tertullian used terminology which he borrowed from the law—*substance* and *person*. In the Trinity, he said, there is one substance shared by three persons.

This idea is similar to the modern legal doctrine of joint ownership, which is difficult both to explain and understand, but which has the utmost significance in modern real property law. According to this doctrine, if three persons own a piece of land jointly they each own all of it, so that if two of them were to die, the third is automatically considered the full owner of the property.

Tertullian's understanding of substance and person in the Trinity approximates this doctrine. For him *substance* was in a sense the "property owned" jointly by the three divine persons. That is, each member of the Trinity "possesses" divinity entirely, so that each person is fully divine while still fully distinct from the other two persons. As we will discover, the ease with which the Western Church accepted Tertullian's formula stood in marked contrast to the Eastern Church's struggle to hit upon a satisfactory formula.

Notice that Tertullian does not approach the relationship between Father and Son in the same way that Justin had. For Tertullian the incarnation was the key element of Christian belief, and thus Platonic quibbling over how the Father and the Son could be of equal divinity didn't affect Tertullian. He never asks the question, "How does the incarnation work?" He simply comes up with a formula to express a truth which must be accepted in faith. This was characteristic of the way Westerners approached the incarnation and the Trinity. Eastern thinkers, on the other hand, with their Platonic bent, plunged fully into the inner workings of these mysteries, trying to explain "how they worked." In the pages ahead we will see how the differing approaches—the Eastern and the Western—had great influence on the shape of early Church history.

Let's look now at the two most influential Eastern apologists. Clement of Alexandria (c. 150-215) and Origen (c. 185-254) were much more than apologists. Yet there was a strong apologetical thrust to their writings, which we will consider here.

Clement of Alexandria

Like Justin, Clement taught that many of the ancient philosophers had known Christ before Jesus. Like Justin, he also found the source of this knowledge in the revelation of the preexistent *logos*. Clement goes farther than Justin, however, by asserting that philosophy was to the non-Jews what the law was to the Jews—the means by which both peoples will eventually be brought to Christ. Thus in Clement's estimation such persons as Plato or Socrates are to be considered on a par with Israelite prophets like Elijah or Isaiah.

The core of Clement's apologetics was his teaching on the relationship between faith and reason. Clement believed both that "faith is to be known" and that "knowledge is to be believed." Clement saw faith and reason on a continuum. Faith serves as the philosopher's "first principle," upon which all logical propositions are based; and knowledge serves to inform one's faith. When Thomas Aquinas in the 13th century defined theology as "faith seeking understanding," he was but restating Clement's own principle.

Like Justin before him, Clement showed no reluctance in criticizing philosophy's errors when those errors conflicted with revealed truth. Plato said that God composed material creation through the work of an intermediary called the *demiurge*, whose "raw material" consisted of preexisting forms. If Clement had followed Plato on this, he would have come squarely into conflict with the biblical view that God himself—directly—was the author of creation. Clement criticized philosophers like Plato for "deifying the universe," rather than acknowledging that "God alone made it, because he alone is God in his being. By this sheer act of will he creates; and after he has merely willed, it follows that things come into being."[7]

Clement challenged the pagan philosophers precisely at the point where reason had to yield to faith. If God has *will*, then the ancient pagan belief in fate and chance is overthrown. There is a "who" in charge of the universe rather than an "it." In the last analysis, then, Clement based his argument to the pagans on Christianity's fundamentally unique characteristic: God is a *person*, who has fully revealed the nature of his personhood both through Scripture and through the incarnate *logos*.

Origen

Origen was one of the few apologists who had been born a Christian. (Most apologists had converted to Christianity after long searches among the various schools of philosophy.) Origen's father, Leonidas, had been martyred in 202. The story is told that Origen's mother had to hide her son's clothes in order to prevent him from turning himself in to the authorities in order to follow in his father's footsteps.

Origen's greatest contribution to early Christian thought is his work on the Bible. In the *Hexapla* he set forth in six parallel columns the Hebrew Old Testament, his own Greek transliteration and the four most popular Greek versions of the time. For Origen the study of Scripture was the "art of arts" and the "science of sciences."[8] Origen developed scriptural exegesis into a true academic discipline. He was the first significant Christian Bible scholar, and he taught that there were three levels of meaning in Scripture— the literal, moral and spiritual.

Although Origen never doubted that Scripture was literally true, his own Platonic predispositions eventually lead him to doctrines which later theological reflection judged as opposed to normative Christianity. For example, Origen stated that the doctrine of a literal resurrection was "preached in the churches for the simple-minded and for the ears of the common crowd who are led on to live better lives by their belief."[9]

The true meaning of Scripture concerning the resurrection—what Origen called the "spiritual sense"—was that "in the body there lies a certain principle which is not corrupted"[10] which gives rise after death to a new type of spiritual body. This "certain principle" was the eternal, preexisting soul. Here Plato's doctrine of the preexistence of the soul brought Origen into sharp conflict with the Church's belief both in God's creation of the soul out of nothing and the physical resurrection.

Origen's principal apologetical work is his *Against Celsus*. The philosopher Celsus was a virulent anti-Christian writer who engaged in rabid attacks against the Church (see page 28). Since Celsus' *True Discourse* (c. 178) preceded Origen's most productive period (218-230) by nearly half a century, the famed apologist at first thought he would simply let Celsus' attack die a peaceful death. Eventually, however, he was persuaded by friends to take up his pen in defense of the faith. The result was the most famous *apologia* of the early Church.

Celsus' attack against Christianity focused on the concepts of grace and forgiveness. To educated and refined pagans it was morally repugnant to hear Christians claim that God forgave the rankest (and, it was implied, the most *uneducated*) sinner. Celsus mocked the Church's claim that "whoever is a sinner, whoever is unwise, whoever is a child and, in a word, whoever is a wretch, the kingdom of God will receive him."[11]

Origen upheld without compromise—as the gospel's core teaching—the doctrine of God's free election of sinful humanity. However difficult it may be for pagans to accept this and other Christian teachings, he proclaimed, the truth of the gospel must be upheld. "We tell no incredible tales," he wrote, "when we explain the doctrines about Jesus."[12]

By Origen's death in 254, Christian apologists had gone a long way toward reconciling faith and reason, revelation and speculation. Yet a most vexing question remained unanswered: "How is it exactly that God became man, and what is the relationship between the God-man and the supreme, absolute One from whom the God-man comes?" In Chapter Four we shall see how this unanswered question bursts forth into the first great crisis of early Christianity. But first we need a little more background information.

The dialogue between Christian revelation and pagan philosophy discussed in this chapter had two simultaneous effects: On the one hand pagan thinkers, through the apologists' explanations, were often influenced to accept the truths of Christian revelation. At the same time the Christian revelation, when expressed in philosophical terms, lost some of its original simplicity and vigor. Some of these new pagan converts failed to appreciate the radical change in belief that Christianity demanded, and they tended to cling to their old beliefs while professing to accept Christianity. Thus a new phenomenon arose: *heresy*.

We turn now from the dialogue between Christians and avowed

non-Christians to the dialogue between people all of whom *profess* to be Christian. For the early Church *this* dialogue proved more perilous than the confrontation with pagan philosophy had ever been.

6

CHAPTER THREE

RULE OF FAITH

Christians Confront One Another: The Rise of Heresy

T here were many streams of heresy flowing within and about the early Church. Trying to reconcile faith and reason and to explain the inner workings and the significance of the incarnation, thinkers took a little bit of this and a little bit of that from the great systems of ancient philosophy. Unlike the apologists, those judged heretics forced bizarre thought systems on the Christian revelation and, in doing so, prevented any true reconciliation between faith and reason. Worst of all, they turned the incarnation into a monstrous new creation which obliterated the key teaching of revelation, that God had truly become a man.

In this chapter we shall look at heresy up until the time of Constantine—the same time frame covered in Chapter One. We shall condense our discussion into three main categories: (1) Gnosticism, (2) the teachings of Marcion and (3) heretical doctrines growing out of the early Trinitarian debates. Then we shall look at the Church's developing criteria to test the orthodoxy of Christian teaching.

GNOSTICISM: CHALLENGE FROM WITHIN

The Church's greatest challenge in these early centuries was neither persecution nor criticism by pagan intellectuals. By far, the most deadly threat to the early Church's continued existence was a school of thought known as Gnosticism. Because Gnosticism often successfully disguised itself as normative Christianity, it threatened to subvert the Church's teaching authority from within.

Gnosticism was a perverted, jumbled and uninformed version of Platonism. We could think of it, perhaps, as the uneducated person's Platonism.

Those Gnostics who considered themselves Christian often lived within the mainstream of the Christian community, some of them perhaps not even realizing that their views stood in radical opposition to the gospel. Remember, the new convert from paganism in the early second century did not yet have a "New Testament" to read. He or she had to rely on the oral teachings of people professing to represent what the Apostles said. It was not always easy for the new convert to know who to believe, or whose argument made the most sense.

Gnostic leaders claimed to be the only authentic proponents of the gospel and accused the Christian bishops of having distorted Jesus' teaching. For the neophyte Christian it was often very difficult to know who truly proclaimed the gospel and who did not.

Key Concepts

Before discussing how the Church met the Gnostic challenge, let's first get a clearer understanding of Gnosticism itself. Although there were many different types of Gnosticism, often advancing opposing viewpoints, we can isolate several key elements in the general structure of Gnosticism as it existed during the days of the early Church.

Dualism. In Gnostic thought, God and the world were radically opposed to each other. God, conceived of by each of the Gnostic sects in a slightly different way, was generally believed to be a deity of the utmost purity and transcendence. (Notice the similarities here to Platonism.)

Somehow, however—either through accident or evil trick, depending on the particular sect—the supreme God lost his divine fullness (called the *pleroma*). As a result, lesser deities came into existence who in turn produced material creation. Each of these lesser deities (called *aeons*) inhabited and ruled its own realm of existence. The farther these realms were from the *supreme* God, the less godlike (and thus less pure) they were.

The Demiurge. The evil god which carried out the process by which the supreme God's fullness slipped away from him was the *demiurge*. In their bizarre fashion, the Gnostics generally associated the demiurge with Yahweh (God of the Old Testament) who, they said, created the world for evil and selfish motives. Thus, for the Gnostics the demiurge (or *creator God*, Yahweh) was evil and perverse and inferior to the *supreme*, unnamed God. The demiurge, Yahweh, created six vassal lords to serve him. These were called *archons*, and each ruled a "heaven." Thus, including the demiurge's own realm, there were seven heavens separating the world from the supreme God. (I realize that this is all starting to sound like *Star Wars* or some other modern-day science fiction, but hang in there.)

Human Beings. For purposes of vanity the archons decided to "make man after *our* own image" (cf. Genesis 1:26—thus the Gnostics accounted for the plural in this verse). In creating humanity the archons unwittingly injected into the human spirit a share of the supreme God's divine spirit (*pneuma*) which they themselves possessed.

This is where the great struggle began. The supreme God—seeing in humanity this spark of his own divinity—contrived some means to allow humanity's share of *pneuma* to escape from imprisonment in the human body and return to the *pleroma*. Yahweh and his dark lords, of course, strove to prevent the supreme God from doing this, seeking instead to perpetuate their narcissistic creation.

Gnosis and Salvation. The word *Gnosticism* is derived from the Greek for "knowledge." Gnosticism acquired this name because of its essential teaching: One becomes free of the body's confinement and returns to the supreme God only through a secret *knowledge*, or *gnosis*. This knowledge is revealed only to a select few by messengers from the supreme God who secretly skirt through the seven heavens to bring truth to humanity.

These messengers may *look* like human beings, but they really only take on the *appearance* of human flesh in order to accomplish their missions. (Hence the heresy of *Docetism*, from the Greek word for "appear." More on this later.) The Gnostics generally believed that there had been four messengers in human history: Buddha, Zoroaster, Jesus and Mani. (This Gnostic conception of Jesus as "messenger" is perhaps the most commonly held view of Jesus among today's educated Americans under 30 who consider themselves religious. To see what I mean, take a look at the "metaphysical" section of any modern bookstore.)

Salvation for a Gnostic consisted in receiving from the divine messenger secret passwords which enabled the human soul after death to pass through each of the seven heavens and return to the supreme God, where the soul then merged back into the deity. In this way God would eventually recapture his lost fullness. The seven dark lords become enraged upon learning that the messenger has outwitted them, so they do all in their power to prevent humanity's salvation—its "release" and "escape" from matter and the world.

The Gnosticism of Valentinus

We can add flesh to this skeletal outline by briefly describing the thought of Valentinus, who flourished from 135-165. His system was the most popular one which the early Church confronted.

The name which Valentinus gave to the supreme God was Bythos. The thought of Bythos is called Silence. Together, Bythos and Silence produce 30 aeons, the last of which is Sophia (Wisdom). From Sophia eventually comes the demiurge—Yahweh, the God of the Old Testament—who, in his ignorance, thinks himself to be the supreme God and thus creates the universe.

The demiurge (Yahweh) creates three types of human beings: (1) the elite *spiritual*, who by nature are destined for salvation; (2) the ignorant *material*, who are forever trapped by material creation and thus doomed; and (3) the *psychic*, for whom there exists a choice for either salvation or perdition. It is this latter group to whom Jesus was sent with the secret *gnosis*.

Irenaeus: Gnostic Fighter

Although several early Christian thinkers, such as Tertullian and Hippolytus, wrote anti-Gnostic treatises, the Church's greatest opponent of Gnosticism was Bishop Irenaeus of Lyons (c. 130-200). Probably born in Smyrna, Irenaeus studied in Rome and was ordained a priest in Lyons in southern Gaul. While he was in Rome to visit with Bishop Eleutherius in 177, Irenaeus's congregation back home suffered a severe persecution. When he returned to Lyons he succeeded the martyred Pothinus as bishop. Irenaeus's major work was his treatise *Against Heresies*, directed principally against Valentinian Gnosticism.

As we have seen above, the starting point for all Gnostic error was the distinction made between God the creator (Yahweh, the evil demiurge) and the supreme God (God the savior). Irenaeus's first challenge was to destroy this distinction and to show that the creator God and the savior God are one, and that this one supreme God was the very Yahweh of the Old Testament whom the Gnostics abhorred.

Irenaeus did this by writing of the "two hands" of God. By this metaphor Irenaeus refers to the Son and the Holy Spirit. It is through them—and not through the Gnostic Yahweh—that God has both created and saved the world. Yet Irenaeus makes it clear that neither the Son nor the Spirit are intermediary gods; they are each fully divine.

Contrary to the Gnostics, Irenaeus maintains the fullness of God's divinity throughout both the creative *and* redemptive processes. He thus addressed the great dilemma which so vexed the Greek apologists and which was to continue to vex Eastern Christian thinkers:

How could God be one and transcendent and yet incarnate in the world?

For Irenaeus, a Westerner, this was never a problem. Through the Son and the Spirit God's unity and transcendence are preserved at the very time that God in Jesus is saving and redeeming the world. Irenaeus realized that if God had not truly become man in Jesus, then humanity was not really ennobled and raised to a new level of existence. To express his view of the significance of the incarnation from *humanity's* point of view, Irenaeus wrote that "the glory of God is man fully alive!"

This explanation attacked Gnosticism's false view of humanity as inherently evil. Whereas the Gnostics interpreted "God's image" in Genesis 1:26 to mean the image of the seven dark lords, Irenaeus wrote that the full image of God resides only in the Son. Accordingly, human beings are created in God's image insofar as they grow into Christ (following Ephesians 4:13).

It is interesting to note here that Irenaeus did not believe that Adam and Eve possessed preternatural powers (such as freedom from suffering and death) before the fall. Instead of *returning* to a state of godlikeness, Irenaeus sees humanity as *growing into* that state through Christ. Perhaps Irenaeus reached this conclusion in order to get away from the Gnostic emphasis on humanity's "return" from earth to God. For Irenaeus, then, Adam's fall was not a fall from grace but a detour from the orginal path to perfection.

The method by which God returns humanity to this path is Christ's work of "recapitulation," or "summing-up." By this Irenaeus means that Christ sums up in his own human experience the experience of fallen humanity. Instead of repeating all of humanity's sins and errors, however, Christ perfects humanity at each stage of his own personal history. Thus, for example, whereas Adam gave in to temptation and *sinned*, Jesus resists the devil's temptation in the desert and *heals* the wound given humanity by Adam's sin.

In this way, Adam's fault is corrected and humanity is restored to the path of righteousness. Through recapitulation, Irenaeus wrote, Christ has "assimilated himself to man and man to himself."[1] Irenaeus sees salvation, then, as the process by which Christ unites himself to humanity. The incarnation is as much a salvific act as is the crucifixion, since it is in Mary's womb that Christ first took sinful human nature into his own.

Through his doctrine of recapitulation Irenaeus effectively defeated the Gnostic challenge. He showed salvation not to be an "escape" from evil matter but the very divinizing of matter. For Irenaeus, Christ is hardly the "messenger" of the Gnostics. Christ comes not to reveal secret wisdom, but to take humanity upon himself. In doing this he does not *appear* to be a man, he actually *is* a man.

In the growth toward God which Christ makes possible, individual humans do not *lose* their identity—as is the case with the Gnostic merger of the soul into the "supreme God"; rather, individuals fulfill and maximize their unique identity in the eternal divine-human union. With Irenaeus's refutation of Gnosticism, the early Church could read with renewed confidence the Scripture passage which asserted, "God looked at everything he had made, and he found it very good" (Genesis 1:31a).

MARCION AND HIS RIVAL CHURCH

After Gnosticism, the most serious heretical challenge to confront the early Church was the teaching of Marcion. Whereas the Gnostics infiltrated the established Church, Marcion—something of a Gnostic himself—formed a rival organization. The Marcionite associations were supervised by bishops who ordained priests, and they worshiped with virtually the same liturgy used by the established Church (which had been called the "Catholic Church" by anti-heretical writers ever since Ignatius of Antioch had coined the term in the year 105).

Marcion founded his church sometime after 140, the year he had first arrived in Rome from his native Sinope, a port city on the Black Sea in today's Turkey. Marcion's father was Bishop of Sinope and had excommunicated Marcion from the Church for his immorality. Marcion brought to Rome the fortune he had made in the shipping business, and he began to ingratiate himself with Christian congregations in Rome by giving them huge donations of money. Gradually Marcion began to preach his own brand of Christianity. As Marcion's views became better known, the Roman Church recognized them as obvious heresy. Bishop Pius I (140-155) formally excommunicated Marcion in 144.

Marcion taught the dualistic nature of God, that Jesus only *appeared* to be human (see above, p. 39), and that the human body was evil. Like other Gnostics, Marcion denied that the God of the Old Testament was the supreme God. According to Tertullian, Marcion taught the existence of two gods, "one judicial, harsh, mighty in war; the other mild, placid, and simply good and excellent."[2] The first was the creator-god, Yahweh, the God of the Old Testament. The second was the Supreme One of the Gnostics who sent Jesus into the world. Irenaeus said that Marcion considered Yahweh, to be "the creator of evils, lustful for war, inconstant in his attitude and self-contradictory."[3]

Marcion concluded that Christianity, being the revelation of the true "supreme" God, was a religion of love; while Judaism, based on belief in Yahweh the creator-god, was a religion of law. Love, or grace, was the means of salvation, while law was but a means of servitude to Yahweh. Marcion rejected the entire Old Testament and accepted from the early Church's writings only Paul's letters (except the Pastorals) and Marcion's own edited version of Luke's Gospel. 7

Marcion rejected the other three Gospels because he felt they were shot through with Jewish propaganda concerning the Old Testament God. Any positive reference in Paul's letters to the law (for example, Romans 7:12)—Marcion said—were later Jewish additions to the text. (Marcion and all Gnostics exhibited a strong anti-Jewish bias.)

Marcion was not the first, nor would he be the last, to distort Christianity by setting "love" in opposition to responsibility. Paul himself had been confronted with this false dichotomy. Some early Christians misinterpreted Paul's gospel of grace to mean that in Christianity there existed absolute freedom to do as one pleased.

Paul had made it clear, however, that the freedom won for humanity by Christ was a freedom which entailed great responsibility for others. Marcion, on the other hand, distorted what Paul meant by love and grace so that these became purely selfish concepts. For Paul, freedom in Christ meant freedom *for* acts of loving service; for Marcion it meant freedom *from* constraints, so that one could gratify to the utmost one's own desires.

Tertullian best summarized Marcion's views when he said, "Marcion's special and principal work was the separation of the law and the gospel."[4] Marcion wanted to point Christianity in the direction of Gnostic mysticism, totally stripping Christianity of its this-worldly—its incarnational—value. Once again we see an effort to remove the great "stumbling block," the core Christian teaching, "The Word became *flesh* and made his dwelling among us" (John 1:14, emphasis added).

Marcion's heresy was in one sense a blessing in disguise for the early Church. Prior to Marcion the Church had not arrived at a consensus as to which books should be included in the New Testament. Indeed, at this point there *was* no New Testament. The versions of inspired Christian Scripture varied widely from place to place. Some bishops had thought that the *Didache* (see p. 11) was inspired Scripture. Other early works competing for inspired status in the minds of the bishops included the letter written by Clement of Rome to the Corinthians (from which we quoted in Chapter One, p. 8), and the various letters of Ignatius of Antioch.

Because Marcion rejected so many of the generally accepted Christian writings, the Church was challenged to determine which of these writings it was going to authenticate as inspired. The Church began to scrutinize these writings more closely and to measure them against its most reliable norm of orthodoxy—the Apostles' teaching. It found this apostolic teaching preserved not only in writings but in its own oral teaching and in its everyday belief as lived out by ordinary, "everyday" Christians. These "little people" did not participate in lofty theological debates, but they professed their Christianity through a type of love that Marcion would not have understood.

The ultimate criterion for a writing's acceptance into the New Testament, then, became its compatibility with the Church's vision of itself as the repository of apostolic authority, as verified by the ordinary Christian's lived faith in the incarnation. The process of sorting out the various writings took centuries. Down to the sixth century, for example, the *Didache* was in many places still considered an inspired New Testament work. A true consensus on the New Testament literature did not emerge until well after the close of the period covered in this book.

THE FIRST TRINITARIAN DEBATES: BISHOP AGAINST BISHOP

The Gnostics and Marcion had challenged the Church's belief in the incarnation. They also challenged the Church's apostolic authority as it resided in the person of the bishop. Thus, not only did they attack Catholic doctrine, they attacked the Catholic Church itself as an organized structure. Now we reach a different conflict. For the first time we find *bishops* arguing among themselves about the meaning and significance of the incarnation.

The Monarchian Controversy: Reacting to Subordinationism
Monarchianism draws its name from the word "monarchy," which suggests the doctrine's central concern—to emphasize God's unity and oneness.

We have seen how Christian apologists stressed the role of the preexistent *logos* in the history of salvation. (See Justin and Clement, p. 30 and p. 33.) Because of their emphasis on the *logos*, some apologists tended to *subordinate* the Son to the Father, making the Son "less divine" than the Father. They were undoubtedly influenced by the philosophical concepts, even though they tried to distinguish between the Christian *logos* and the pagan concepts of lesser, intermediary gods.

As the apologists' writings circulated throughout the Church, some Christians foresaw the dangers to which this "Subordinationist" tendency could lead. If the Son was not of equal divinity with the Father, then Christianity had turned right into Platonic dualism. Because of this fear, some opponents of Subordinationism became *Monarchists*, that is, they overreacted by emphasizing the *unity* of God to the exclusion of his individualized personhood.

Two types of Monarchical thinking developed: Adoptionism and Modalism. These are difficult to comprehend and to explain, but these two distinctions within Monarchianism are essential to our understanding of the future course of early Church history.

Adoptionism: The first type of Monarchianism derived its name from the Greek word *dynamis* (meaning power) and was thus known as *Dynamic Monarchianism*. Proponents of this school of thought said that Jesus was an ordinary man in whom God's power operated in an extraordinary way. Jesus' divine nature was thus all but denied.

Dynamic Monarchianism is also known as *Adoptionism*. Some of its proponents believed that at some point in Jesus' life, such as his Baptism in the Jordan, God "adopted" Jesus by giving him divine power. This school of thought differs from Subordinationism in that the latter sees Christ as a god of lesser status—but a god nonetheless. Dynamic Monarchianism, or Adoptionism, by contrast, sees Christ as merely a man, but a man "permeated" as it were with God's power.

Perhaps an analogy will help us to see the distinction between Subordinationism and Monarchianism. Subordinationists "pushed" God's divinity *down* on a graded scale of being, while Dynamic Monarchists "concentrated" God's essence strictly within the Godhead, suspicious of letting that essence come into contact with the world.

Modalism: The second form of Monarchianism was *Modalistic Monarchianism* or, for brevity, *Modalism*. Within this viewpoint the one God exhibits different *modes* of behavior—one mode being represented by the Father, another by the Son and the third by the Holy Spirit. Thus any distinctions in the Trinity are transitory and dependent upon how God wants to operate at a given time. In Modalism God was certainly one, yet he was able to function as any one of three persons at a given time.

The first Modalist was Praxeas, against whom Tertullian had written (see p. 32). For Praxeas, Father and Son were so completely united in the Godhead that it was accurate to speak of the Father as having died on the cross. Because of this view, *Modalism* was given the nickname *Patripassianism*, literally the belief that "the father suffers."

The most famous early Modalist was Sabellius, who expressed his views in Rome during the time of Bishop Zephyrinus (199-217). (Because Modalism had become so associated with Sabellius, many Christian writers simply called Modalism *"Sabellianism."*) Bishop Callistus (217-222) eventually excommunicated Sabellius.

Let's pause to straighten out this confusing picture by studying the following chart:

Subordinationism

Christ the *logos* is a "lesser god" than God the Father.

Dynamic Monarchianism—Adoptionism

Christ is only a man in whom God's power operates in an extraordinary way. God "adopted" Christ at some point in the latter's adult life.

Modalistic Monarchianism—Modalism—Sabellianism

The one God appears now as Father, now as Son, now as Holy Spirit. These three "modes of behavior" are not distinct persons. When Christ died on the cross the Father suffered.

Wrangling Over Words

The Modalist heresy led to a controversy between two bishops named Dionysius: Dionysius of Rome (259-268) and Dionysius of Alexandria (247-264). The latter had been a student of Origen and had directed a famous Christian catechetical school in Alexandria from 233 until 247. About the year 260, he wrote certain letters in which he condemned Modalism, but his language raised eyebrows in Rome. He called Christ *poiema*, the Greek for "creature." Dionysius of Rome wrote to his namesake in Alexandria asking for clarification.

In his letter the Roman bishop implied that his Alexandrian counterpart believed in an exaggerated Origenism (the philosophy of Origen which flourished after his death). Certain Origenists in the East used the Greek term *hypostasis* to refer to the three persons of the Trinity, but it was not always clear that they actually meant "person" by *hypostasis*. (What the word really does mean has been the subject of endless debate.) Among these Origenists at times the word *hypostasis* seemed to mean "nature," and thus for them to say that God had three *hypostases* bordered on saying that he had three different natures.

Such an interpretation would mean that there are really three different Gods in the Trinity. Dionysius of Rome, by associating Dionysius of Alexandria with this Origenist school of thinking, did in fact suggest that his brother bishop in Alexandria might be a closet "tritheist" (believer in three Gods).

The Roman bishop insisted that the *unity* of God must be safeguarded. In doing so he injected into the debate a Greek word which was to have immense significance for the future: *homoousios* (pronounced "hahm-ah-ou-see-ahs") meaning "of the same substance," from the Greek words *homo* (same) and *ousia* (substance). For Dionysius of Rome, one could be orthodox only by saying that Christ was *homoousios*—of the *same* substance with—the Father.

The dispute was complicated by the fact that in the West the Greek word *hypostasis* was translated by the Latin word for *substance*, which, as we have seen, was the West's terminology for the common divinity of the three persons (see p. 32). Thus, in the West when Christians heard the Easterners say "three *hypostases*," they thought it meant that Easterners believed in three "substances" or three different Gods. Many Westerners thought the Easterners were Subordinationists.

In the East, on the other hand, the Latin word *persona*—person—was translated into Greek as *prosopon*, which could mean "face" or "mask" as well as person. When Eastern Christians heard that Westerners believed in "three *personas*" in one substance, they imagined that Westerners were saying that the one God simply had "three faces," which is of course Modalism. Let's avail ourselves of another chart which, I hope, will make things clearer.

	Greek East	Latin West
Hypostasis (Greek)	For some writers this word seemed to connote "nature." If so, then "three *hypostases*" suggested "three Gods."	Westerners used "three *personas*" instead of "three *hypostases*."
Persona (Latin)	In Greek, this was translated as *prosopon*, which could mean "face" or even "mask." Were the Westerners saying God wore the three "masks" of Father, Son and Spirit?	Westerners said "three *personas* in one *substantia* (substance)." They translated *substantia* into Greek as *-ousia* rather than as *hypostasis*.
Homoousios (Greek) —the stem *ousia* means "being," "essence" or "substance."	"Of the same substance" suggested to certain Greeks blatant Monarchianism, i.e., one *hypostasis* only, not three.	"Of one substance" safeguarded the Church from the heresy of tritheism—three separate Gods.

This chart and the preceding discussion help to explain why Dionysius of Alexandria, when writing back to the Roman bishop, refused to compromise on the Eastern usage of "three hypostases." To the Alexandrian bishop such a usage was proper and orthodox. Actually, he may have understood *hypostasis* to be close to what the Latins meant by *persona*. In his response, Dionysius of Alexandria also criticized his Roman brother's use of *homoousios* by reminding him that the word was found nowhere in Scripture.

Thus the two bishops—their respective protests to the contrary notwithstanding—each came away from the dialogue believing the other to be a heretic. The Roman bishop suspected his Alexandrian confrere to be a Subordinationist, and the latter thought the Bishop of Rome to be a Modalist.

We might be tempted to ask at this point, "Why did these two bishops make such a big deal about words? Why couldn't they just love each other as Christian brothers and overlook the 'small stuff'?" Try to put yourself in their shoes. They lived in a time when many Christians had grave doubts about what normative Christianity really was. As bishops, both Dionysiuses saw it as their responsibility to proclaim authentic Christian teaching. To do this, they had to use words. Thus for them the dispute over words was not petty squabbling but the essence of authentic evangelization. As they might have put it, "It does no good to proclaim the gospel if we proclaim it erroneously."

NORMS OF ORTHODOXY

Because of the kinds of conflicts over the meaning of the incarnation which we have just discussed, the Church by the third century was becoming adept at recognizing heresy. As a result, the Church developed certain criteria by which it hoped to distinguish orthodox from heterodox teaching in the future. These criteria were (1) the doctrine of apostolic authority, (2) the New Testament canon and (3) the "rule of faith."

Apostolic Authority

The heretics *selectively* chose which apostle to follow and which not to follow. For example, Marcion rejected all but Paul's teaching (and accepted only portions of that), while Valentinus emphasized only the Gospel of John. The Catholic Church, however, stressed the necessity of accepting the entire body of apostolic teaching. Irenaeus proudly reminded his readers that "Peter was an apostle of the very same God as Paul was."[5]

The New Testament Canon

The word *canon* comes from the Greek for "measuring rod," and has come to mean norm or rule. As we saw in discussing Marcion, the New Testament canon developed alongside the doctrine of the Church's continuing apostolic authority. Irenaeus wrote of the progression from the apostles' oral teaching to their written words, calling the latter "pillar and bulwark of our faith."[6]

For the early Church, then, it was impossible to separate Scripture and apostolic authority, or tradition, into two separate categories as is done today. To the early Church, Scripture *was* tradition and tradition lived on in Scripture. To a Christian of the second and third centuries it would have made no sense to ask whether one accepted Scripture only, or Scripture *and* tradition. Such a question acquires meaning only in a much later era of Church history.

The 'Rule of Faith'

This phrase, used by both Irenaeus and Tertullian, refers to short summaries of the core Christian belief which began to develop early in the second century in response to heresy. These rules of faith were the forerunners of the great written Creeds which developed in the second half of the Church's early period, and which we will discuss beginning with the next chapter. The anti-heretical writers insisted that these rules were an unshakable guide to apostolicity and thus to normative Christianity.

Beginning early in the second century, every Christian congregation, in no matter how small a town, possessed a "rule of faith" by which it expressed the essential truths of Christianity in ordinary everyday language. These rules of faith were the "bottom line" of Christian belief, the means by which the "little people" in the Church influenced the great theological debates. No matter how profound and abstract later debates over the incarnation were to become, few bishops wanted to depart from the core beliefs as expressed in these rules of faith.

While rules of faith differed from place to place, all preserved what Origen called "the particular points clearly delivered in the teaching of the apostles."[7] These points were: Father, Son, Holy Spirit, and Jesus' life, death and resurrection. The best early example (c. 140) of a rule of faith is a document known as "R"—short for "Ancient Roman Symbol." (In the early Church, *symbol* was another word for Creed.)

R, like many rules of faith, was originally phrased as a set of questions asked of baptismal candidates. The text of R was as follows:

Do you believe in God the Father almighty?
Do you believe in Christ Jesus, the Son of God,
Who was born by the Holy Spirit from the Virgin Mary,
Who was crucified under Pontius Pilate, and died,
and rose again on the third day living from the dead,
and ascended into the heavens,

and sat down on the right hand of the Father,
and will come to judge the living and the dead?
Do you believe in the Holy Spirit,
in the holy Church?*

The important point about R for our purposes is this: Well before
Nicaea (the ecumenical council which produced the first great Creed in
325), the early Church had already decided that a "rule of faith" existing
separate and apart from Scripture was an essential means of defining
normative Christianity. The first two criteria of normative Christianity
were subject to vicissitudes. Christians could differ over their
interpretation of Scripture. And when bishops themselves disagreed over
key elements of the faith, the only unfaltering criterion of normative
Christianity became the rules of faith and their descendants, the great
Creeds.

In the Introduction the question was posed: Which was more
important in the method the early Church used to define the truths of
Christianity—thought or belief? The rules of faith are a "handle" by
which to grasp this question. While normative Christianity as defined by
the great Creeds owes much to the *thinking* of Christian intellectuals, a
great debt is also owed to the *belief* of the average Christian as
summarized in the primitive rules of faith, as we shall see.

No orthodox thinker in the early Church—no matter how great his
intellectual powers—desired to depart from the basic Christian beliefs
contained in the rules of faith. As we enter into the great intellectual
discussions about the incarnation in the pages ahead, we must never
forget that in the back of each great thinker's mind was the sense of the
Christian belief summarized by the "little people" in their rules of faith.
Thus, in the great Creeds of the fourth and fifth centuries (which we still
cherish today), we are in touch with great mental achievement and, at the
same time, we are in touch with the everyday faith of the humblest early
believer.

THE CHURCH ON THE EVE
OF THE ARIAN CONTROVERSY

The early Church's experience in confronting both philosophy
(Chapter Two) and heresy (Chapter Three) brought it to a much deeper
insight into the truths of the gospel message.

First of all, the Church came to understand more clearly than
before the significance of the incarnation. Platonism and Gnosticism
urged Christians to seek the "pure spiritual life" by escaping from this
"lesser" existence of the flesh. But the Church held fast to its belief in the

essential goodness of God's creation.

The incarnation meant that God in his very person had sanctified humanity for all eternity. Salvation thus consisted not in denying one's material nature, but in glorifying that nature through means of the divine energy released into the universe at the resurrection. "The glory of God is people fully alive!"

Secondly, through its conflict with Marcion the Church came to understand that "love" without responsibility is no love at all. True Christian love is not a mystical *experience* which removes one from the troublesome here and now; love, the Church proclaimed, is essentially a *decision* to follow Christ to the cross by dying for one's brothers and sisters.

In the early days of Christianity when the pagans exclaimed, "See how those Christians *love* one another!" they were not observing the conduct of escapists whose first priority was their own peace and affluence. They saw the Christians' love manifested in their hospitals and orphanages, in the generous support which they gave to widows, in the hand which they offered to the weak and infirm, and in their willingness to accept joyfully the lowly place to which society had relegated them.

Finally, after the disagreement between the two bishops named Dionysius, the Church realized that episcopal authority was not an infallible guide to normative Christianity. Something more was needed. The developing Christian New Testament was insufficient to serve as that "something more" since learned and holy men often gave to the same Scripture passages diametrically opposite meanings. More and more, then, the Church yearned for a uniform and universal "rule of faith" similar to those which individual congregations throughout the Empire had already been developing as an essential element in the bedrock of Christianity.

As the Church moved into the age of Constantine, its desire for a great Creed would be fulfilled—but at a tremendous cost to its own sense of identity and purpose!

CHAPTER FOUR

OF ONE SUBSTANCE WITH THE FATHER

Crisis of Belief and the First Catholic Creed

The rules of faith may have been sufficient for local congregations, but until all Christians everywhere could have a universally applicable rule of faith—a Catholic Creed—individual congregations could still differ over the meaning and significance of the incarnation. In this chapter we will examine the crisis of belief (the Arian controversy) which forced the Church to formulate a universal, normative expression of the meaning of God-become-man (the Nicene Creed). First, some background information on how the Chuch reached this crisis point.

THE FIRST YEARS AFTER CONSTANTINE

It is not difficult to imagine a persecuted Church watching in amazement as Emperor Constantine marched into battle under a Christian banner. Nor is it difficult to understand why Christian writers characterized the days following Constantine's conversion in the most glorious of terms.

The Church historian, Bishop Eusebius of Caesarea (c. 260-340), recorded the Church's memory of the years following Constantine's conversion. In his *Church History*, Eusebius called Constantine a "great light and deliverer," and "God's beloved." Much of what we know about the peaceful and prosperous halcyon days in which the Church first experienced the favor of the Empire comes from Eusebius's pen.

Eusebius, known as the "Father of Church history," is important both for his own writings and for preserving the writings of many other early Christian thinkers. While studying in Caesarea under Origen's disciple Pamphilus (240-309), Eusebius began to catalogue his teacher's library (c. 280). Distracted by the subject matter of the manuscripts which he handled, he stopped and read every book. In his later writings he refers to many of these books and quotes sections from them. Since most of the originals of Pamphilus's library have been lost, Eusebius is our oldest source today for many of the early Christian writers and for much of early Church history.

Constantine: Initial Euphoria

Eusebius quoted Constantine's own analysis of his rise to power: "God wanted my service and regarded as appropriate the carrying out of his resolve."[1] Most other bishops at first did not detect a threat to the Church's independence in Constantine's words. Ten years after Constantine's conversion, however, many bishops were wondering whether God wanted Constantine's service to the degree in which the emperor offered it.

In the first years after his conversion, Constantine's assistance to the Church was truly a wonder to behold. He restored all confiscated property and prohibited pagan officials in his government from offering sacrifice to the gods. What's more, he placed himself squarely behind the Church's moral teachings by imposing restrictions on divorce and by outlawing the gladiatorial games.

Gradually, in every conceivable way, Constantine showed the pagans that he regarded the state religion with contempt. Particularly insulting to the pagans was the emperor's act of destroying the pagan temples and transporting their religious artifacts to his new capital (Constantinople), where he displayed these artifacts not as religious relics, but as museum pieces of a bygone age.

Having debased pagan religious art, Constantine then became the great patron and sponsor of Christian architecture and art. His great ambition was to make of Christian Palestine a land of Christian shrines. Over the site of Jesus' burial he built a great basilica, taking pains to instruct the architects how to decorate the building's facade. At the site of the Ascension he built a second basilica, and in Bethlehem, a third, the Church of the Nativity.

Constantine raised the money for these projects by taxing his Eastern governors. Just 10 years after they had been instructed by Diocletian to administer the most barbarous cruelties to the Christians, they must have thought it strange they were now ordered by Constantine to open the state purse to the Christians. In all of these building activities the local bishops took a back seat. Constantine made it clear that he, and not the bishops, was responsible for the new direction of Church architecture.

Constantine slowly began to see himself as a key participant not only in external Church matters such as architecture, but in the Church's purely religious affairs as well. The first occasion for Constantine's intrusion into theological debate concerned the Donatist controversy in North Africa.

Donatism: Sign of the Crises to Come

In the East, where Diocletian's persecution had been particularly harsh, Christians tended to take more of an all-or-nothing attitude about their relationship with the Empire. Either one was an apostate or a potential martyr; there was no middle ground. In the West, on the other hand, where Diocletian's persecution often had been carried out with little fervor, Christians were divided over the question of how much contact with the State was proper.

The division in the West over this question led to the Donatist schism. Mensurius, Bishop of Carthage (the leading Christian city of North Africa), had cooperated with Roman authorities during the persecution. Although he was not a "*traditor*"—one who "handed over" Church books to the Roman police—during the height of the persecution Mensurius followed Roman orders to cease celebration of the Mass and other public worship.

When Bishop Mensurius died, his deacon, Caecilian, was consecrated Bishop of Carthage (311-345). One of the North African bishops who consecrated Caecilian not only had prohibited the liturgy in his diocese, but had even been a *traditor*, handing over Mass books and Bibles to the police for burning. Such conduct was looked upon as a sacrilege by other bishops in North Africa who, like their brothers in the East, had taken a very firm stand on the question of collaboration with the Roman persecutors.

Caecilian's consecration by an "apostate" bishop infuriated the rigorist Bishop Majorinus from Numidia, an area of North Africa where the rigorist position was dominant. The bishops of Numidia, in order to counter Caecilian's installation as Bishop of Carthage, consecrated Majorinus as bishop of that see. Caecilian eventually secured Constantine's support, and it was only this support which enabled him to keep his office. The emperor was saddened and confused by the quarrel between two groups of Christians. In Constantine's mind, being a recent convert, all Christians thought alike and peaceably agreed on every issue. It was a rude awakening for him to discover that there were deep divisions within the very Church which he hoped to use as a force to unify the Empire. Constantine realized that only his office and authority could negotiate a truce between the two sides of the dispute.

The Church in Rome and in the rest of the Mediterranean came out in support of Caecilian. Bishop Miltiades of Rome convened a council in 313 which deposed Majorinus—Caecilian's opponent. Donatus (after whom the schism was named) succeeded Majorinus as rigorist bishop of Carthage and appealed the Roman Church's decision directly to Constantine.

The emperor personally appointed a group of bishops to meet at Arles in France to review Bishop Miltiades's decision. When in 314 the Council of Arles upheld Miltiades' decision, Constantine—reluctantly but forcefully—once again brought the power of the State down upon the heads of Christians by repressing the heretical Donatists. (As we shall see in Chapter Eight, Constantine's repression of Donatism was ineffectual. It was not until the issue could be fully debated theologically that Donatism died out as a competing Church in North Africa.)

No one in the Church questioned Constantine's authority to convene bishops for the settlement of a religious controversy. Indeed, most bishops saw Constantine's action as a sign of God's favor and blessing. Looking back on the early days of Constantine's rule with historical hindsight, we may perhaps question the bishops' facile acceptance of Constantine practically as fellow bishop—a title, incidentally, which Constantine once used to refer to himself.

In judging these earliest days of Church-State *rapprochement*, however, we should keep in mind both the horror which the Church had experienced under Diocletian and, ironically perhaps, the respect with which all citizens of the Empire—Christians included—regarded the office of the emperor. Even during the worst persecutions, Christian writers such as Tertullian and Origen had praised the Roman state as the protector of order and the channel of God's blessing.

DIFFERING THEORIES OF CHURCH AND STATE

The early Church, even before Constantine, had gradually developed a theory of Church-State relationship which saw the Empire's destiny and the Church's destiny as being inextricably intertwined. By Constantine's time Christians had long come to think of the Empire as the earthly means by which God would propagate and nourish his Church. By the time Constantine began to assert himself as the bishops' "senior partner," few Christians doubted that Constantine's interventions in

Church affairs were anything but a manifestation of God's will.

Eusebius of Caesarea, for example, in seeking to develop a theological model by which to comprehend the relationship between Church and State, called the Empire the *icon*, or image, of heaven. As heaven has only one Lord, so too the earth has one sovereign—its emperor who serves in the divine Father's stead until the earthly kingdom merges into the heavenly one at the end of time. The emperor, then, is God's *vicar* on earth.

In Eusebius's mind, the Church was identical with the Empire. This identity is summarized in Eusebius's phrase, "Christian Roman Empire," an entity which for Eusebius defines and brings into fulfillment the Kingdom spoken of in the Gospels. And, as any kingdom can have only one monarch, the sovereign ruler of the Christian Roman Empire must be the emperor, who according to Eusebius is "a sort of universal bishop."[2]

Following the Easterner Eusebius's theory, the Eastern Church came to regard Constantine as the "equal of the Apostles." The Western bishops, however, were more cautious in their evaluation of the emperor's achievements. This differing approach signified what was to become two divergent perspectives on the relationship between Church and State.

The Eastern Church was never able to free itself from imperial supervision. In the West, however, the growing authority of the Bishop of Rome (and of strong bishops in other cities such as Ambrose of Milan) acted as a counterbalance to imperial control of Church affairs.

By the end of our period, East and West had devised two different solutions to the question of Church-State relationship: The Eastern Church, with its theory of "Caesaropapism," had virtually indentured itself to the emperor. The Western Church and its papacy competed with and eventually came to dominate the emperor in all matters affecting Church life. (We will take up the development of the Western Church and the papacy in Chapter Eight.) As we shall see, these two differing attitudes on Church-State relationship were already developing when the Arian controversy began. They were to influence the way in which all future theological debates unfolded during the remainder of our period.

Early in Constantine's rule, the bishops of *both* East and West made scarcely a whimper of protest against the emperor's gradually increasing power in Church affairs. (Their acceptance of Constantine's role in the Donatist controversy is a case in point.) By Constantine's death in 337, however, with the Arian controversy raging like an unstoppable conflagration, more and more bishops, especially in the West, were beginning to have second thoughts. By letting the imperial nose into their tent, had they committed themselves to bringing in the rest of his body as well?

THE ARIAN CONTROVERSY

With the Arian controversy we reach a pivotal point in the early history of Christian thought and belief. At stake was the incarnation itself. The Church had to decide once and for all if it really believed that God had become man and, what is more, whether it would practice this belief by proclaiming, as Irenaeus had, that with the incarnation humanity itself had been raised to a new, *divinized* level of existence. Let's see how the Arian drama unfolded.

Arius was born about the year 250, probably in Libya. He had been a deacon in the diocese of Alexandria. Bishop Peter of Alexandria (300-312) had excommunicated Arius for being a member of the Melitian sect, a Christian group which took a very rigorist position on the readmittance into the Church of Christians who had lapsed during Diocletian's persecution. When Bishop Peter died, however, his successor, Bishop Achillas, ordained Arius a priest (c. 313). Shortly after 313, Alexander became the new bishop of Alexandria. He learned that there was a popular young priest in his diocese named Arius who had attracted quite a following while preaching a somewhat unusual doctrine about the second person of the Trinity.

Alexander scheduled an open discussion and called upon Arius to present his views publicly. The ordinary Christian in the East was always eager to listen to someone's speculations about the incarnation. Easterners had an insatiable appetite for theology (and for theological controversy). Since the Church did not yet have an official, universal teaching on the incarnation, many people were simply trying to come to a better understanding of the incarnation by listening to as many viewpoints as possible.

According to the fifth-century Church historian, Sozomen, Arius stated his position to Alexander as follows: "The Son of God was created out of non-being, there was a time when he did not exist, according to his will he was capable of evil as well as virtue, and he is a creature and created."[3] On another occasion Arius stated, "The Son who is tempted, suffers, and dies, however exalted he may be, is not to be equal to the immutable Father beyond pain and death; if he is other than the Father, he is inferior."[4]

Given the uncertainty of great thinkers such as Justin (see p. 30) with regard to the relationship of the Son to the Father, it is not surprising to find Arius espousing the crudest type of Subordinationism. What is surprising is the degree of support which Arius found for his position, particularly among bishops. This shows us that even many bishops had not yet concluded what the incarnation really meant. Although Bishop Alexander excommunicated Arius in 321, he discovered that by doing so he had touched only the tip of the Arian iceberg.

Arius had no intention of withdrawing quietly, but instead sought episcopal support for his teachings. His first supporter was Bishop Eusebius of Nicomedia (not the same person as Eusebius the Church historian). This Eusebius eventually emerged as the leading Arian bishop of the early fourth century.

For some years Nicomedia had been the Eastern imperial capital. Since Constantine and his family maintained a summer palace and court there, Eusebius was Constantine's pastor and a close family friend. It was he who baptized Constantine on his deathbed in 337. By gaining Eusebius's patronage, Arius had instantaneously transformed an Alexandrine theological squabble into a debate that occupied the entire Church.

When Bishop Alexander (back in Alexandria) received the distressing news that Eusebius had come out in defense of Arius, he convened a synod of over 100 Egyptian bishops. The synod excommunicated all clergy in Egypt and Libya who supported Arius. The battle had been joined.

Arius opened a school in Nicomedia hoping to spread his ideas to other bishops. Bishop Eusebius of Nicomedia wrote a circular letter for Arius addressed to all Eastern bishops urging them both to denounce Alexander and the actions taken by the Egyptian synod, and to pressure Alexander to receive excommunicated Arian clergy back into the fold. Arius for his part was quite a propagandist. He composed jingles and rhymes which made it easier for the less educated to learn and accept his doctrine.

Alexander responded to Eusebius's letter with an encyclical of his own, which he likewise sent to all Eastern bishops. At least 200 of these bishops expressed their support for Alexander. In Rome, Pope Sylvester I (314-335) first learned of the Arian controversy through the dust stirred up by the two episcopal letters circulating in the East. For the time being, however, the Western Church thought little of the controversy and did nothing to enter the fray.

It was about this time that Constantine also first learned of the controversy. The emperor had appointed the Spanish Bishop Hosius of Cordoba as his theological adviser. Had Constantine selected an Eastern rather than a Western adviser, his whole understanding of the theological issue at stake in the Arian controversy no doubt would have been much different, and the entire course of Church history likely would have been altered.

Hosius was a respected intellectual who had proven his faith by undergoing torture and imprisonment during the latter stages of Diocletian's persecution. Constantine sent Hosius to Alexandria to look into the controversy involving Arius and to report his findings upon returning to Constantinople. The emperor sent a letter with Hosius in which he expressed his naive hope to bring the quarrel to a quick conclusion.

At this early stage of the controversy, Constantine understood neither the theological complexity of the argument nor the ingrained hostility of the disputants. The bishops of Alexandria and Constantinople were jealous and suspicious of each other, and thus there is no doubt that ecclesiastical politics had a role to play in the Arian controversy.

Upon Hosius' return from Alexandria, however, Constantine became soberly apprised of the depth and magnitude of the split between the two camps. Perhaps following Hosius' advice, Constantine decided that only a great council of bishops could settle the matter. Before we consider the Council of Nicaea, however, we should first analyze in more detail the doctrinal dispute which led up to it.

Arian Theology

The core of Arian theology taught that Christ—the eternal "Word" (John 1:1)—was at some point created by the Father, and thus not of equal divinity with the Father. Arius had written, "Before (the Son) was begotten or created or ordained or established, he did not exist." [5] In this way Arius sought to preserve God's absolute oneness and indivisibility. The Arians could not conceive of a God in three persons who was at the same time the monotheistic God of Scripture. For them, the doctrine of the Trinity was but veiled tritheism (belief in three Gods). Why not admit the obvious, they said, and speak of the Son (and the Holy Spirit) as being created and derivative from the Father?

Arianism, then, was but one more attempt to transform Christianity into Platonism with its series of intervening gods and its belief that the supreme, transcendent God somehow was opposed to created matter. Over and over again the early Church confronted this kind of effort to denigrate creation in favor of a "spiritualized" reality, safe from humanity's debasing touch.

The Arians simply could not bring themselves to believe that the supreme, absolute God actually became human. To accept this doctrine meant admitting that humanity itself had become ennobled and dignified—and that humanity was inherently lovable by the Creator. Arianism clung to the Platonic world view in which God was an "it" and not a "who." They could not make the leap of faith to believe in a God who truly loved his creation.

The Arians' view of God naturally affected their view of salvation. Since for the Arians Christ was a creature, he did not possess divinity in its fullness. Thus, any moral virtue which Christ exhibited arose from his own will rather than from his divine nature. Jesus, therefore, could have freely chosen to perform evil. Yet, the Arians said, God "foreknew" that Jesus actually would not sin, and thus—by anticipation—God allowed Jesus on earth a "share" in the divine life in which all persons could one day participate. For the Arians, then, Jesus did not redeem anyone by his death on the cross, nor did he defeat death and sin. He simply showed others by his own perfect example how they too could earn salvation.

Despite their understanding of salvation, the Arians continued to address prayers to Jesus and to baptize in the name of the Father, Son and Holy Spirit. Orthodox writers like Athanasius of Alexandria (296-373) belittled the Arians for their inconsistency in calling Jesus a creature on the one hand and worshiping him on the other. Because the Arians' external devotions did not differ greatly from Catholic worship, many uninformed people had difficulty distinguishing between Catholicism and Arianism.

The Arians became great missionaries and converted many of the barbarian peoples to Arianism. When these peoples later encountered Catholic missionaries, they saw little reason for changing their beliefs. Not until the Franks *forcibly* converted the Arians to Catholicism in the early Middle Ages did Arianism die out.

THE COUNCIL OF NICAEA

In order to settle the Arian controversy, Constantine invited bishops of East and West to assemble at Nicaea in the province of Bithynia, a city which lay about 75 miles due south of Constantinople across the Sea of Marmora. To underscore the earnestness of his desire for as many bishops as possible to attend, Constantine provided free transportation for the 318 bishops who eventually did attend the Council.

Only *five* Western bishops heeded the emperor's call; all the remaining bishops were from the East. The names of only two of the Western bishops are known: Hosius of Cordoba, who in addition to serving as Constantine's adviser also may have acted as the pope's representative at the Council, and Caecilian of Carthage (see p. 55).

The leading Eastern bishops in attendance (and the key protagonists in the drama) were, on the Catholic side, Alexander of Alexandria, Eustathius of Antioch, Marcellus of Ancyra and Macarius of Jerusalem. The leading Arian spokesmen were two bishops of the same name—Eusebius of Nicomedia and Eusebius of Caesarea, the Church historian. (The latter Eusebius seemed to be a "tentative" Arian, not really staunchly advocating Arianism as did his namesake from Nicomedia.)

The Council opened on June 19, 325, in the emperor's palace. First the bishops were seated facing each other along the imperial hall. Then the emperor strode into the hall and seated himself on a golden throne at the head of the hall. After giving the bishops a lengthy lecture on his principal objective in convening the Council—the restoration of peace and unity among the bishops—Constantine sat back to watch the debate. (The emperor, although exerting pressure on the bishops to come to unanimous agreement, nonetheless allowed them to debate their views freely and openly.)

The Arians opened the debate, but it soon became evident that their position was not the majority view. It became obvious to all that the central issue for deliberation was not *whether* the Arian position would be defeated, but *how* the bishops would word the majority declaration.

The Arian Bishop Eusebius of Caesarea offered his local Baptismal Creed (the local "rule of faith" for the Church in Caesarea) as the definitive formula of orthodoxy, telling the bishops, "As we received from the bishops before us, both in our catechetical instruction and when we were baptized..., so also we believe now and submit our belief to you."[6]

There is some question as to whether Eusebius was actually proposing a definitive formula for settling the Arian controversy or simply trying to convince everyone of his disputed orthodoxy. At any rate, the text of Eusebius's local rule of faith was as follows:

> We believe in one God, the Father, almighty, maker of all things visible and invisible; And in one Lord Jesus Christ, the Logos of God, God from God, light from light, life from life, Son only begotten, *first-begotten of all creation*, begotten before all ages from the Father, through Whom all things came into being; Who because of our salvation was incarnate, and dwelt among men, and suffered, and rose again on the third day, and ascended to the Father, and will come again in glory to judge living and dead; We believe also in one Holy Spirit.[7] (Emphasis added.)

Most bishops present wanted to accept this wording as expressive of orthodoxy, but certain anti-Arian bishops were not satisfied. For them,

Eusebius's formula was not explicitly anti-Arian, and some phrases within it were openly suggestive of Arian doctrine, e.g., such words as "first-begotten *of all creation.*" These bishops moved for an entirely new formula—in fact, for an official Catholic Creed that would definitively state a position on the incarnation that would apply to all Christians everywhere.

At this point, Bishop Alexander's deacon, the young Athanasius, emerged as the most articulate spokesman for the Catholic position. As Athanasius himself reported it, the bishops tried mightily to find a scriptural formula that would express the Catholic view of the Son's equal divinity with the Father. Yet, each time the Catholic bishops proposed such a formula, the Arians twisted the interpretation of the proposed scriptural passage so that it supported their own doctrine. In the end it became obvious that there was only one solution—the use of the unscriptural but also unambiguous *homoousios*, which expressed the belief that the Son is of the same substance as the Father (see p. 46).

As we shall see momentarily when we quote the Nicene Creed in its entirety, the bishops incorporated other phrases into the Creed which specifically were intended to be anti-Arian. For example, the bishops referred to Christ as "*eternally* begotten of the Father, God from God, begotten, not *made,*" as well as, of course, "of one substance" (*homoousios*) with the Father. (The Church today translates this phrase as "one in *being* with the Father.")

All but two of the Arian bishops at the Council—Secundus and Theonas—yielded to Constantine's plea for signatures, and thus the new Creed came into existence. As revealed by their subsequent actions, however, Eusebius of Nicomedia and other Arian sympathizers no doubt crossed their fingers as they signed.

The Nicene Creed
The text of the Creed which the bishops signed is as follows:

We believe in one God, the Father, almighty, maker of all things visible and invisible; And in one Lord Jesus Christ, the Son of God, begotten from the Father, only-begotten, that is, from the substance of the Father, God from God, light from light, true God from true God, begotten not made, of one substance with the Father, through Whom all things came into being, things in heaven and things on earth, Who because of us men and because of our salvation came down and became incarnate, becoming man, suffered and rose again on the third day, ascended to the heavens, will come to judge the living and the dead; And in the Holy Spirit. But as for those who say, there was when He was not, and, before being born He was not, and that He came into existence out of nothing, or who assert that the Son of God is of a different hypostasis or substance, or is subject to alteration or change—these the Catholic and Apostolic Church anathematizes.[8]

'The Homoousion'

The crowning achievement of Nicaea was the *homoousios* formula (theologically called "the homoousion"). However, since the breakup of the Nicene accord (which we discuss in the next chapter) and most later doctrinal debate revolve around this term, we would do well to analyze the homoousion in more detail.

The great problem with the homoousion was that it admitted of several different meanings. Its root, *ousia*, could mean "substance," but also "being," "essence" and "reality." To compound the difficulty, *ousia* was sometimes used as a synonym for *hypostasis*, which, as we saw in Chapter Three, was another ambiguous word, sometimes used to mean "person."

At Nicaea many of the bishops accepted the homoousion only because they felt free to place their own interpretation on it. Eusebius of Caesarea, for example, said that for him the term meant only that "the Son of God bears no resemblance to creatures, but is in every way *like* his Father who begot him."[9] This distorted translation clearly compromised the true meaning of *homoousios*. Had the bishops wanted to say that the Son was *like* the Father, there was another Greek word which they would have used: *homoiousios* ("of *like* substance"; notice that an "i" is inserted in this word before the third "o" of *homoousios*).

The bishops' uneasiness over the homoousion had much to do with ecclesiastical politics and the growing division between the Western and Eastern Churches. More than likely it was the pope's representative, Hosius of Cordoba, who sold Constantine on the use of *homoousios*. Athanasius, some years after Nicaea, wrote that "it was Hosius who put forth the faith accepted at Nicaea."[10]

Even though the West had sent only five bishops to Nicaea, it was Western theology which become the Council's dominant position in the end. This fact troubled many Eastern bishops who went home grumbling to themselves that the emperor had replaced Arius's Subordinationism with the West's Sabellianism (or Modalism; see pp. 45-46). Many Eastern bishops felt that by accepting a Creed which said that the Son was "of the same substance" with the Father, the Church was denying the *distinction* between the Son and the Father which belief in the Trinity presupposed.

Yet, as other Eastern bishops began to reflect on what had happened at Nicaea, they came to see that the homoousion was in fact the best possible expression of the Church's traditional belief.

64

Only by asserting that the Son was of the same substance with the Father could the Church uphold its belief in the Son's dual role as creator and savior.

As we saw earlier, the core of the early Gnostic heresies had been the separation of God into two Gods—one creator, one savior. In the homoousion the Church rejected this false dichotomy. Only if Christ is "of the same substance with the Father" can God's creative and salvific activities be united, and this is precisely why the homoousion eventually came to be accepted as a badge of orthodoxy. Bishop Amphilochius of Iconium (c. 340-395) summed up the significance of the homoousion when he wrote that "a man is altogether irreligious and a stranger to the truth if he does not say that Christ the Savior is also the maker of all things."[11] The root problem with Arianism was that it made Christ a creature and not creator (in contradiction to one of the key truths of the Christian revelation; see Colossians 1:16).

The key to understanding Nicaea's use of the homoousion, then, is contained in the words of the Creed itself:

> Who because of us men and *for our salvation* came down and became incarnate.

Only God can save humanity; only God can make humanity God-like. This is what the bishops at Nicaea sought to affirm as a central doctrine of Catholic Christianity.

Seeds of Discord

The Nicene synthesis contained within itself the seeds of future discord. For one thing, a unity imposed by the emperor could only be superficial, and could last only so long as the emperor continued to support the homoousion.

Second, many bishops were uneasy with the synthesis. According to the interpretation given to the homoousion by some bishops, the term too closely identified Father and Son. These bishops concluded that the Church's official teaching was now Sabellianism. These bishops felt deceived by the Council's achievement. The Council's announced purpose had been simply to define the divinity of the *Son*, and not to adopt a formula which *equated* the Son with the Father (which is the way they understood *homoousios*).

The Catholic bishops associated with Bishop Alexander of Alexandria, on the other hand, felt that the Creed did not go far enough in affirming the divine unity. These bishops had wanted to go to even greater lengths to safeguard the divine unity against Arian

Subordinationism, and they gradually developed a deep suspicion of the bishops who expressed caution about the implementation of the homoousion.

Finally, the Arian sympathizers at the Council, who signed the Creed begrudgingly, continued to interpret the homoousion as they chose. As soon as the Council closed they began to filter their way into the emperor's private counsel, intending to subvert the Creed and to destroy the delicate unity which it had effected. It became obvious to everyone that Church "unity" was in a precarious condition.

CHAPTER FIVE

THE LORD AND LIFE-GIVER

From Nicaea to Constantinople

Y ou might consider this to be the "ups and downs" chapter of the book. We will discuss how the Catholic position at Nicaea was overthrown by an Arian resurgence, how the Arians came up with their own Creed, and how the Catholic position eventually retriumphed at the Council of Constantinople in 381. The events of this period are complicated and confusing, and it's very difficult at times to tell which side is "up" and which "down."

This chapter is largely concerned with great theological issues. You may feel like asking along the way, "What happened to the ordinary Christians? Did they 'hibernate' while the great intellectuals debated fine points of theology?" No, ordinary Christians did not disappear from view. They followed their bishops' debates about what the incarnation meant—and tried to live the gospel in the midst of a very confusing time.

If you think the years following Vatican II have been confusing and unsettling to the average Catholic, imagine what it must have been like between 325 and 381. As bishops heatedly debated the key doctrine of Christianity—the incarnation of God in human flesh—the average Christian must have felt like saying, "If our own bishops can't agree on what the incarnation means, what are we supposed to think?"

Although we follow the debate in this chapter through the recorded *thought* of great intellectuals, the *belief* of the "little people" hung in the balance. They watched the debates with great interest, and because of their *sense* of the Christian revelation they intuitively gravitated toward and supported the eventual orthodox position. It was no accident that the great mass of believers between 325 and 381 supported the Catholic champions—men like Athanasius, Basil the Great and the two Gregorys. It was no accident that these great thinkers were so popular among the common folk. The "little people's" faith gave assurance that the *thought* of the great intellectuals was correct.

Let's sketch briefly the flow of events, thought and belief between the Councils of Nicaea (325) and Constantinople (381).

THE UNDOING OF NICAEA

Shortly after Constantine sent the bishops home from Nicaea the leading Arian bishop, Eusebius of Nicomedia (not Eusebius the Church historian), revealed his true colors and revoked his support of the Creed. Constantine was furious, and sent Eusebius into exile. Yet in 328, for reasons that are unclear, he brought Eusebius back and reinstalled him as bishop of Nicomedia. From that point on the wily Eusebius wormed his way into power and eventually became the emperor's theological adviser. (Hosius of Cordoba had returned to Spain at the close of the Council.)

It became Eusebius's unalterable goal to undo the achievement of Nicaea. He sought to do this both because he was a dedicated Arian and because he was jealous of the prestige which the see of Alexandria had gained from the Alexandrians' triumph at Nicaea. Church politics now becomes as important to our story as theological issues.

Instead of attacking the Nicene Creed, which would have enraged Constantine, Eusebius instituted a program of character assassination against the leading Nicene bishops: Eustathius of Antioch, Athanasius of Alexandria and Marcellus of Ancyra.

Eusebius first stirred up a whispering campaign against Eustathius. He eventually confronted the emperor with a catalogue of Eustathius's alleged moral vices, and accused the bishop of Antioch of public disrespect to the emperor's mother. Constantine allowed a synod of bishops to be convened to investigate the charges, and this synod deposed Eustathius.

Eusebius then decided to move against Athanasius, who had succeeded Alexander as bishop of Alexandria in 328. Constantine was persuaded to call another synod to investigate certain trumped-up charges which Eusebius made against Athanasius. This Synod of Tyre (335) was a complete travesty of justice. Athanasius was allowed to present no bishop to speak on his behalf, while the Arians skillfully orchestrated Athanasius' condemnation and verdict of deposition. Although Athanasius appealed personally to the emperor, Constantine honored the synod's decision and exiled Athanasius (the first of four exiles during his lifetime).

The final Nicene defender to be deposed was Marcellus, bishop of Ancyra. Here Eusebius had an easy task. Marcellus went around making statements which confirmed the suspicions of many moderate Catholic bishops that the homoousion was a code word for Sabellianism. Apparently Marcellus taught that the Son and the Holy Spirit "emerged" from God simply to take part in creation and redemption. At the end of time when there would be no more need for their activities, they would collapse back into God's absolute unity. Marcellus was a great embarrassment to Athanasius and had no real support among other bishops. With the two leading moderates, Eustathius and Athanasius, deposed, Marcellus's deposition followed as a formality at the Synod of Constantinople in 336.

The doctrinal field was now dominated by the Arian party. Constantine went so far as to call Arius himself out of exile, but he died before his excommunication could be officially lifted.

A year later (337) Constantine died. Imperial rule was divided among his three sons: Constantine II, Constantius II and Constans. Constans became co-emperor in the West and a dedicated Nicene supporter. Constantius II became co-emperor in the East and an ardent Arian. (The third brother died shortly after his father.)

When Constantine died, Athanasius quickly returned to resume leadership of his flock in Alexandria. But as the Arian Eastern emperor, Constantius II, gained power he hastily arranged for an Arian named Gregory from far-off Cappadocia to be ordained bishop of Alexandria.

The Christians of Alexandria revolted for two reasons: They loved Athanasius, and they had always elected their own bishop. By force of armed guard, however, Constantius sent Athanasius back into exile (exile number two).

When the unpopular Arian Bishop Gregory of Alexandria died in 345, Constantius allowed Athanasius to return to his see. To the Arians' chagrin, Athanasius came home to a hero's welcome, boasting that he could count over 400 bishops who supported him and Catholic Nicene theology. Yet 400 Catholic bishops could not outweigh one Arian emperor and a handful of Arian bishops.

In the West when Constans died in 350, the Arian Constantius became sole emperor. His Arian bishops instituted a fanatical campaign against Athanasius. Constantius called a synod which met at Arles (in France) in 353. The only item on the agenda was a decree condemning Athanasius, which all but two bishops were coerced into signing. Constantius and his Arian bishops felt that if they could get rid of Athanasius and his keen theological insights, they could reestablish Arian theology once again.

Having gotten the vast majority of the Catholic bishops to sign his decree condemning Athanasius, Constantius could now take direct action against the Nicene champion. He sent a troop of soldiers to Alexandria where they entered a church to arrest Athanasius while he was assisting at a liturgical service. As members of his flock literally laid their lives down between the soldiers and their bishop, Athanasius escaped and fled to the Egyptian desert (exile number three—356). It was during his desert period that Athanasius began to write those works which would mark him as the Church's leading Nicene theologian.

The Arian Creed

With Athanasius temporarily out of the way, the Arian bishops persuaded Constantius to convene an entirely new council to revoke the Creed accepted at Nicaea in 325. Even though Constantius had been able to coerce most of the Western bishops to depose Athanasius, he was clever enough to realize that the Western bishops were still overwhelmingly pro-Nicene and anti-Arian. He agreed to a new council only on the condition that the Eastern and Western bishops meet in separate locations. In this way he hoped to control the events to his advantage. Accordingly, the Western bishops met in the Northern Italian town of Rimini, and the Eastern bishops in Seleucia (today's southeastern Turkey).

Following a complicated series of intrigues on the part of the Arian bishops, and ruthless coercion by Constantius, nearly 400 bishops of the West and 150 of the East gave their consent to a new Arian Creed.

The substance of this Arian Creed had been worked out by the Arian Bishop Acacius of Caesarea. Acacius wanted to get away from the troublesome *ousia* altogether and proposed the doctrine that the Son is *like* the Father (not of like *substance* with the Father, just "*like*").

Those bishops who supported Acacius were called Homoians, from the Greek word *omoios*—"like." Although the Homoians may not have gone to the same lengths as Arius had to establish that the Son was of less divinity than the Father, it was nonetheless obvious that they were thoroughgoing Arians. They refused to profess that the divine Word had existed eternally with the Father. It was this new Homoian position which Constantius forced on both groups of bishops, through intimidation and bullying, and which was formally ratified at a synod in Constantinople in 360.

The Homoians' Creed now became the formal doctrinal position of the Catholic Church, completely annulling the Nicene Creed of 325. Pertinent portions of this Arian Creed read as follows:

We believe in one God, the Father, almighty, from Whom are all things; And in the only begotten Son of God, Who was begotten from God before all ages and before all beginning, through Whom all things came into existence, visible and invisible, begotten only-begotten, alone from the Father alone, God from God, *like* the Father who begot Him according to the Scriptures, Whose generation no one knows save alone the Father Who begot Him.

But as for the name "substance," which was adopted simply by the fathers, but being unknown to the people, occasioned offense, because the Scriptures themselves do not contain it, it has pleased us that it should be abolished and that no mention at all should be made of it henceforth, since indeed the divine Scriptures nowhere have made mention of the substance of Father and Son. Nor indeed should the term hypostasis be used of Father and Son and Holy Spirit. But we say the Son is *like* the Father, as the divine Scriptures say and teach. But let all the heresies which have either been condemned previously, or have come about more recently and are in opposition to this creed, be anathema.[1]

Notice that only the first paragraph of this "Creed" reads like a Creed. The second paragraph was simply propaganda for the Arian cause. Whereas the purpose of the Nicene Creed had been to formulate a universal doctrine on the incarnation, the purpose of the Arian "Creed" was broader: to humiliate the Nicene bishops and to establish the Arian faction as supreme.

No one knew what "like the Father" in this Arian Creed really meant. Whatever it meant, it was a far cry from Nicene theology. Athanasius, still in hiding in Egypt, sent a circular letter to all the bishops of Egypt urging them not to sign the Arian Creed. The Egyptian bishops were the only group within the Church who refused to offer its allegiance to the new doctrine. Nonetheless, the Church was now officially an Arian Church.

Later, when the Latin Scripture scholar Jerome wrote his reflections on the events we have just discussed, he made this famous observation: "That whole world groaned and wondered to find itself Arian."[2]

Julian the Apostate: Blessing in Disguise

Things could not have looked worse for the supporters of Nicaea. Constantius died in 361, however, and was succeeded as emperor by his cousin Julian, who was neither Catholic nor Arian, but a pagan. Julian devoted all of his energies to belittling Christianity and restoring the ancient Roman religion. Julian was wise enough to know that violent persecution of the Church would be counterproductive. Instead he set out to win the minds of the Christians by instituting reforms which placed all state education in the hands of pagan teachers.

When this program bore little fruit he turned his attack against the bishops. Athanasius, whom Julian had initially allowed to return to Alexandria, was exiled for the fourth time. Other bishops, too, were removed from office and sent into exile.

Julian's pagan revival lasted only two years. (He died in 363 fighting the Persians.) According to a later Christian legend, his dying words were, "O Galilean, you have conquered!"[3]

Julian's reign, however, turned out to be a blessing in disguise for the Catholic Church, since on the verge of becoming obliterated by the Arians, Athanasius and his followers were able to catch their breath during Julian's rule and consolidate their position. During Julian's reign Athanasius traveled around the Empire to teach other bishops the fuller significance of Nicene theology and thus convince his brother bishops of the value of that theology. For the first time the Catholic bishops began to understand why the homoousion was central to Christian belief in the incarnation. Let's take a look at Athanasius' theological achievement.

ATHANASIUS: DEFENDER OF CATHOLIC ORTHODOXY

Just as political history between 325 and 381 reads like a biography of Athanasius, so too the history of Christian thought during this period is largely a chronicle of Athanasius' own mental journey. Athanasius was heir to the rich tradition of Christian thought which had developed in Alexandria. He was heavily influenced by Clement, Origen and all the great thinkers who had lived and taught in Alexandria.

The Incarnation
At the age of 24 Athanasius wrote his famous *On the Incarnation* in which he developed the idea that the Logos, by uniting himself with humanity, was restoring humanity to God's own image. This idea had already been developed by Irenaeus, but it was the Alexandrian School which elaborated upon Irenaeus's thought and developed a theology of salvation as *deification*. A century and a half before Athanasius, Clement had written, "The Logos of God had become man so that you might learn from a man how a man may become God."[4] For Athanasius, this idea that the incarnation meant the beginning of humanity's divinization was the core of Christian theology.

This was the key point which neither the Gnostics nor the Arians could accept: that God by becoming man in Jesus Christ had infinitely ennobled and dignified humanity. The incarnation meant that humanity was God's most precious creation, not the evil and base reality the Gnostics and the Arians thought. Athanasius showed how the incarnation verified Scripture's own statement, "...in the divine image he created them" (Gn 1:27).

Athanasius' theology is more practical and less speculative than the thought of his Alexandrian predecessors, partly because Athanasius became so embroiled in controversy, and partly because he wrote not as a scholar but as a persecuted bishop. For Athanasius, theology had to give workaday solutions to vexing dilemmas—and be convincing to people without the time or ability to follow the lofty paths of a Clement or an Origen. He thus provided the Church with a theology that, as far as the average believer was concerned, worked and made sense. Athanasius was the most popular bishop of his day.

Several years before Nicaea, while still a deacon, Athanasius had already developed his thinking on the relationship between Father and Son to such a degree that he would later become the obvious choice as defender of the Nicene cause. In *Against the Heathens* he defined his concept of God's Word as "the God of the universe, the very Word which is God, who while different from things that are made, and from all creation, is the one Word of the good Father, who by his own providence ordered and illumines this Universe."[5]

In this early work Athanasius was concerned with distinguishing the Logos of God from the Stoic concept of the *logos* as a principle of reason within the universe. Yet, at the same time, he anticipates the Arian Subordinationist doctrine by declaring the Logos to be "the very Word which *is* God."

In doing this Athanasius pointed Eastern theology in a new direction, away from the Platonic, Arian Subordinationist viewpoint which saw the Logos as a lesser god, and toward the Western viewpoint developed by Tertullian—three persons in one substance. Because of his Trinitarian writings, Athanasius became (perhaps) the first Eastern theologian whom the Western bishops fully trusted.

During Athanasius' four exiles he was supported by the pope and other Western bishops, and he always found their dioceses to be safe havens. Through Athanasius Western Christians learned of the theological controversies in the East, and they threw their support behind the little bishop from Alexandria who lived as Jesus himself did, with virtually "nowhere to lay his head" (Matthew 8:20).

At Nicaea it was perhaps Athanasius alone who fully understood the significance of the issues debated. He recognized at once that Arianism distorted the apostolic faith in two important ways: It shattered Christian monotheism, and it reduced to nothing the Christian understanding of salvation.

Despite their protests to the contrary, Athanasius realized that the Arians, by making Christ a "lesser god," were really returning to the polytheism of the pagans. If, Athanasius asked, the Father creates a lesser god to help him rule the universe, why cannot this lesser god in turn create other lesser gods (just as the Gnostics taught), so that a whole galaxy of intermediary beings is then created? Where does the process stop? In reality, Athanasius said, the one absolute, transcendent God, in one historical time and place, fully took on human flesh in such a way that fullness of divinity was completely shared by both Father and Son.

Athanasius also recognized the implications of Arianism for the Christian doctrine of salvation. If, as the Arians said, the Son is not of equal divinity with the Creator of the universe, then the Son lacks the power to restore fallen creation to its divine image. Only the Creator can re-create humanity, making humanity over from a sinful condition into a participant in God's own life.

For Athanasius, only God could make humanity Godlike. If Christ is a creature as the Arians said, then God's power to save and restore humanity has not truly entered the world. Jesus' life would be nothing more than a noble example of virtue and wisdom. In reality, Athanasius said, salvation was first and foremost a matter of God's power at work in the world. It was not, as is often proclaimed today, a self-development course in which humanity through its own efforts gains "enlightenment."

The Holy Spirit

At Nicaea the bishops had summarized the Church's inadequate theology of the Spirit in the flat and lifeless assertion, "And in the Holy Spirit" (see the Nicene Creed, p. 63).

The bishops' shallow treatment of the Holy Spirit at Nicaea was explained quite simply by Bishop Amphilochius of Iconium (340-395), writing in 376: "...since the question of the Holy Spirit was not being discussed at the time, they did not go into it at any great length."[6]

As the anti-Nicene campaign developed during the middle decades of the fourth century, however, the role of the Holy Spirit became an integral part of the debate over God's nature. In making the Son an intermediary, created god, the Arians sometimes simply referred to Jesus as an "angel," that is, a *manifestation of* God, rather than God's *incarnation*. Out of this Arian angelology developed the idea that the Holy Spirit likewise was God's angel.

In his *Letters to Serapion*, Athanasius condemned this view and argued that, like the Son, the Holy Spirit is fully God. Because of his pioneering work on the third person of the Trinity, Athanasius is considered the founder of *pneumatology*—the theology of the Holy Spirit. Athanasius died before he could develop this theology for the Church's practical use. That task would fall to the three "Cappadocians" (Basil the Great and the two Gregorys—of Nazianzus and of Nyssa—called "Cappadocians" because they all came from the province of Cappadocia).

Thanks to Athanasius, Catholic theology had reached the point where the relationship between Father and Son had become sufficiently clarified and the Nicene Creed had been accepted as the expression of normative Christianity. We will now look at how other thinkers picked up where Athanasius left off to further clarify the theology of the Trinity.

THE CAPPADOCIANS TACKLE THE HOLY SPIRIT

The story is told about a modern Christian missionary in Japan who was attempting to explain the Trinity to an old Zen master. Once the missionary had finished, the Zen master looked politely at his guest and remarked, "I understand honorable Father. And honorable Son I understand too. Please explain again the part about honorable bird."

Perhaps many Christians have never gotten past the bewilderment of the Zen master. This is because, like the old Japanese sage, we have received our understanding of the Holy Spirit from inadequate models.

Is there really any model we can use to explain the Spirit? Fatherhood is a concept we can grasp. And the Son walked among us. But exactly what or who is the Holy Spirit, who neither took on human flesh nor is analogous to a common human relationship such as fatherhood? Such thoughts must have crossed the minds of Basil and the two Gregorys—the first writers to attempt a serious examination of the nature of the Holy Spirit.

Once the Church understood and accepted why the Son was of equal divinity with the Father, it immediately realized that it could not leave hanging the question of the Spirit's divinity. Otherwise, the same old squabble about "lesser gods" and "divine intermediaries" would start up all over again. Arianism would rear its ugly head again, substituting the Holy Spirit as its new candidate for a Subordinationist god.

Basil the Great (330-379), the oldest of the three Cappadocian theologians, received an excellent education. Forsaking what would have been a promising career in the world, he built himself a small hermitage on the Iris River and devoted himself to a life of prayer and solitude. Others joined him, and a small monastic community developed. (We discuss the origins and development of monasticism more fully in Chapter Ten.)

One of these monks was Basil's younger brother, Gregory of Nyssa. Like Basil, Gregory was a capable classical scholar. Eventually both brothers heeded the call to a more active life: Basil became bishop of Caesarea, Gregory likewise became bishop of Nyssa. Whereas Basil was a great administrator, Gregory was a great speculative theologian and the first great Christian mystical writer.

The two brothers' friend, Gregory of Nazianzus (329-389), also became a monk. Of the three Cappadocians he was probably the most temperamentally suited for the monastic life. Yet he and Basil traveled about preaching together, and Gregory's reputation as a brilliant orator stayed with him all his life.

By the time the three Cappadocians took up their pens on the subject of the Holy Spirit, several bishops had already developed a theology of the Holy Spirit which stood in opposition to Athanasius' thinking. One of these bishops, Eustathius of Sebaste, had been a student of Arius and couldn't make up his mind whether to support Nicaea or to condemn it. Eventually he rejected both the homoousion and Athanasius' teaching on the divinity of the Holy Spirit. By 373 an entire group of like-thinking bishops was following his teaching, and they became known as the *Pneumatomachians* (literally, "those who war against the Spirit").

Basil, in refuting the teaching of these men, pointed the theology of the Holy Spirit in an entirely new direction. Basil believed that much of the difficulty in Trinitarian speculation would be eliminated if people could only understand that those two vexing words, *hypostasis* and *ousia*, mean different things.

Here is the way Basil stated the problem: "Many persons in their treatment of the mystical dogma fail to distinguish that which is common to the *ousia* from the meaning of the *hypostases*. Therefore, to some of those who accept ideas about this subject uncritically it seems just as appropriate to say one *hypostasis* as one *ousia*. On the other hand, those who assert three *hypostases* suppose that it is necessary to assert a division of *ousias* into the same number."[7] (Notice how Basil had turned away from the old debate about Father and Son. We are now moving fully into a discussion of the entire Trinity.)

Basil redefined *ousia* and *hypostasis* in a way that would allow the two terms to be used unambiguously: *Hypostasis* was that in God which admitted of distinction, while *ousia* was that which was general and indefinite. Gregory, then, went on to define the Trinity as three *hypostases* in one *ousia*. This distinction pushed Eastern Trinitarian theology closer to the Western view, so long as the West could be made to understand *hypostasis* as equivalent to "person," and *ousia* as equivalent to "substance." (See the discussion on Tertullian, p. 31.)

With terms more clearly defined, Basil next focused his attention on the nature of the third person of the Trinity. Basil wanted to establish that the Holy Spirit was *homoousios* with the Father and the Son, and thus of equal divinity with them.

Basil saw one proof of the Spirit's divinity in Scripture's use of "Holy" as an inseparable aspect of the Spirit's title. For Basil, the Spirit was holy by nature—that is, a sanctif*ier* rather than sanctif*ied*—and thus divine in nature.

Further, Basil said, the Spirit was divine, because it performed divine actions. Throughout Scripture Basil saw the Spirit manifesting such divine gifts as "foreknowledge of the future…(bestowing) the heavenly citizenship, a place in the chorus of angels, joy without end, abiding in God, and being made like to God—and highest of all, the being made God."[8]

Basil found the ultimate proof of the Spirit's divinity, however, in the Church's baptismal practice. Christ's salvation is brought to humanity "in the name of the Father, and of the Son, and of the Holy Spirit." Basil was so confident of his understanding of the Spirit's divinity that in his own diocese he changed the traditional doxology used at Mass, "Glory be to the Father, *through* the Son, *in* the Holy Spirit," to "Glory be to the Father, *with* the Son, together *with* the Holy Spirit."

Gregory of Nazianzus elaborated upon Basil's thought and described the Trinity in terms of *intercommunion* and *interrelationship* between the persons.

In reality, Gregory said, philosophical concepts cannot define God. Only in the *relationship* between the three persons can one really make any sense of words such as "God's essence" or "God's being," since for God those words only take on meaning when used in a *relational* sense.

Gregory of Nyssa, like his two Cappadocian colleagues, ultimately saw that the difficulty in understanding the Trinity stemmed from the application of finite words and concepts to a God who is infinite. For all three Cappadocians the bottom line of Trinitarian dogma was the liturgy of the Church and the faith of the people. While philosophical concepts could cast light on the Trinity, in the end, as Gregory of Nyssa put it, one had to "guard the tradition we have received from the fathers, as ever sure and immovable."[9] In other words, these three great thinkers, while greatly advancing Catholic *thinking*, did not feel themselves qualified to go beyond Catholic *faith*.

With the Trinitarian theology more fully developed by the

Cappadocians, the Church was ready for a new Creed—one with a more definitive statement concerning the Holy Spirit than Nicaea's brief statement.

THE COUNCIL OF CONSTANTINOPLE

As with the Council of Nicaea, the impetus for the Council of Constantinople came from an emperor—this time Theodosius I ("The Great," emperor in the East from 379-392, and of the entire Empire from 392-395). Although emperor in the East, Theodosius was a Spaniard—and thus sympathetic to Western thinking. He was an open supporter of both Nicene theology and the primacy of the Roman bishop.

In 380 Theodosius issued an edict (joined in by co-emperor Gratian in the West) that all Roman citizens should accept the same Christian faith as professed by Pope Damasus in Rome (366-384) and by Bishop Peter of Alexandria. (Ever since Athanasius had moved Alexandrian theology closer to Rome's, Rome and Alexandria had become representatives of much the same theology.) Theodosius made it clear that only the Catholic Christianity defended by Athanasius and the three Cappadocians was henceforth to be considered normative. This was emphasized as the emperor declared his belief "in the one divinity of the Father and the Son and the Holy Spirit in equal majesty and holy Trinity."[10] If one is looking for a moment at which Christianity becomes the "official" religion of the Roman Empire, the date of Theodosius' edict presents the best possibility.

Early in 380 Theodosius conceived of a second Ecumenical Council—to meet for the purpose of clarifying the issues left unsettled by Nicaea. Yet, as if to frustrate his announced purpose, Theodosius sent letters of invitation only to bishops in the East. Thus it is questionable that the second great council should really be designated "ecumenical" (that is, "worldwide"). There were no official delegates from the West in attendance.

So far as we know, about 150 Eastern bishops did attend, about half of the number in attendance at Nicaea. Included in the list of invited bishops were the *Pneumatomachoi* bishops (see p. 76), although it is unclear how many of them actually attended. We can surmise that an intense debate on the Holy Spirit took place. A few weeks after the council began, the faction of bishops who could not accept the divinity of the Holy Spirit left the assembly.

The Constantinopolitan Creed

The chief work of the Council of Constantinople—its revised Nicene Creed—is perhaps best explained in a letter written by the president of the council, Gregory of Nazianzus:

> We for our part have never esteemed, and never can esteem, any doctrine preferable to the faith of the holy fathers who assembled at Nicaea to destroy the Arian heresy. We adhere with God's help, and shall adhere, to this faith, supplementing the gaps which they left concerning the Holy Spirit because this question had not then been raised. [11]

Gregory's statement helps us to understand how the council participants interpreted their work. The bishops at Constantinople did not see themselves as writing a new Creed; rather, they saw themselves as ratifying the Nicene Creed. Of course in doing this, they greatly expanded and revised the Nicene Creed, particularly to bring it up to date with the recent developments in the theology of the Holy Spirit. Centuries later, because of the close association between the Creeds promulgated at Constantinople and Nicaea, people erroneously labeled the creed of 381 as the "Nicene Creed." The text of the Constantinopolitan Creed—the Creed which serves as the "Profession of Faith" in Catholic liturgies to this day—appears below:

> We believe in one God, the Father, almighty, maker of heaven and earth, of all things visible and invisible; And in one Lord Jesus Christ, the only-begotten Son of God, begotten from the Father before all ages, light from light, true God from true God, begotten not made, of one substance with the Father, through Whom all things came into existence, Who because of us men and because of our salvation came down from heaven, and was incarnate from the Holy Spirit and the Virgin Mary and became man, and was crucified for us under Pontius Pilate, and suffered and was buried, and rose again on the third day according to the Scriptures and ascended to heaven, and sits on the right hand of the Father, and will come again with glory to judge living and dead, of Whose kingdom there will be no end; And in the Holy Spirit, the Lord and life-giver, Who proceeds from the Father, Who with the Father and the Son is together worshiped and together glorified, Who spoke through the prophets; In one Holy Catholic and Apostolic Church. We confess one baptism to the remission of sins; we look forward to the resurrection of the dead and the life of the world to come. Amen." [12]

Let us note several significant differences between the Nicene Creed (N) and the Creed of Constantinople (C) and discuss their implications for the history of Christian thought. (Here we follow Professor Kelly's development in *Early Christian Creeds*, pp. 332-344.)

	Creed of Nicaea	**Creed of Constantinople**
Point One	"Became incarnate"	"Was incarnate from the Holy Spirit and the Virgin Mary"
Point Two	"Will come to judge the living and the dead"	"Will come again with glory to judge living and dead, of Whose kingdom there will be no end"
Point Three	"And in the Holy Spirit"	(a) "And in the Holy Spirit, the Lord and life-giver" (b) "Who proceeds from the Father" (c) "Who with the Father and the Son is together worshiped and together glorified" (d) "Who spoke through the prophets"
Point Four		"…in one Holy Catholic and Apostolic Church. We confess one baptism to the remission of sins; we look forward to the resurrection of the dead and the life of the world to come. Amen."

Point One: This expansion of the Nicene Creed gets slightly ahead of our story. This addition was inserted in order to combat a *Christological* heresy (which we take up in the next chapter) which taught that although Jesus had a human body and soul, his human spirit was replaced by the divine *Logos*. By stressing that the Virgin Mary was Jesus' mother, the council wished to emphasize Jesus' full humanity.

Point Two: This language was apparently added to oppose the teaching of Marcellus of Ancyra (see p. 69). If Christ's kingdom lasts forever, then obviously he does not lose his distinct identity at the end of time; he does not "merge" or "collapse" back into the Godhead.

Point Three: Here the bishops used scriptural language and the theological developments since Athanasius' time to define the Spirit's role.

a) See 2 Corinthians 3:17, "The Lord is the Spirit"; and 2 Corinthians 3:6, "The Spirit gives life."

b) See John 15:26, "The Spirit of truth who comes from the Father." Notice that the Creed does not say, "Who proceeds from the Father *and the Son* as in today's "Profession of Faith" in the Catholic liturgy. The added words, *filioque* in Latin, were amended to the Creed in Spain at the Third Council of Toledo (589). This met with furious resistance from the Eastern Church, which wanted to maintain the original language. We will say more on the *filioque* controversy in Chapter Nine.

c) Athanasius had written that the Holy Spirit "is glorified with the Father and the Son."[13] We also are obviously reminded here of Basil's unique doxology (see p. 77). Notice that the bishops did not profess the Spirit to be *homoousios* with the Father and the Son. They omitted the term, apparently to avoid stirring up any more trouble than was necessary with bishops who had rejected the Holy Spirit's divinity. Perhaps the Council's bishops were wary of repeating the dogmatic warfare over *homoousios* which had followed the Council of Nicaea.

d) See 2 Peter 1:21, "...men impelled by the Holy Spirit have spoken under God's influence."

Point Four: Notice that the Nicene Creed omitted these elements of the ancient rules of faith, such as R (see p. 49), from the final wording of the Nicene Creed; the bishops at Constantinople reinserted them. In doing so they were reasserting the continued importance of local congregations' traditional rules of faith. Or to put it another way, the bishops at Constantinople were honoring in their Creed the ancient faith of the average believer. Once again a great Creed served to harmonize Christian thought and Christian belief.

The acceptance and elaboration of the Nicene Creed by the Council of Constantinople established Nicene theology as the Church's definitive expression of apostolic faith. Arianism was decisively defeated, and a more explicit Trinitarian theology came into being. Yet, barely had the Church terminated its struggle to define the relationship between the persons of the Trinity, when a new and more vociferous quarrel arose.

CHAPTER SIX

'MOTHER OF GOD'

The Debate Shifts: From the Persons of the Trinity to the Personhood of Jesus Christ

W elcome to the most complex period in early Church history and the hardest chapter in this book! In this chapter (and the following chapter) the focus of our inquiry into the key Christian mystery, the incarnation, now shifts from "God's perspective," as it were, to "humanity's perspective." We turn our attention away from the Trinitarian debate and toward the *Christological* controversy. (Christology is the study of Christ's person and the union between his divine and human natures.)

Up to now we have been talking about the relationship between Father, Son and Spirit in the Trinity. Our focus has been on the incarnation's effect on the unity and transcendence of the Father. Now we look at the incarnation from another perspective—that of its effect on the man Jesus of Nazareth. A key question that surfaces in this new discussion is whether Mary is really the "Mother of God" or merely the "mother of Christ."

THE RESIDUE OF ARIANISM

With the Creed of Constantinople (381), the Church firmly rejected Arianism's belief in the subordinate status of the Son (and the Spirit) in relation to the Father. But the Arian fire had not yet been fully quenched. Actually, no one *admitted* to being an Arian after 381. For many Arian supporters, however, accepting the reality of

God-become-man continued to be a serious stumbling block.

The Arians had argued that the second person of the Trinity was not fully divine. Defeated on this front, they now simply reversed the argument: "If the eternal Word was not a lesser god than the Father because of the incarnation, then the man Jesus of Nazareth was never fully joined to the eternal Word, never truly united to God." The Arians were simply advancing their old argument under another guise: that humanity was perverse and base and not worthy of intimate relationship with the supreme God. After all, if *Jesus* had not been truly united to God, there is hardly any chance that the rest of us can be so united.

During the height of the Arian controversy the Catholic bishops may not have detected an ominous warning contained in a statement made by Eudoxius, Arian bishop of Constantinople: "We believe in one single Lord Jesus Christ...made flesh, not made man; for he did not take a human soul...not two natures, since he was not perfect man, but God was in place of the soul in the flesh."[1]

Notice here the shift in emphasis from the *Trinitarian* issue to the *Christological* issue. Eudoxius was not writing about the *external* relationship *between* the persons of the Trinity, but about the *internal* constitution of Christ's own person. He was saying that Jesus was not a "real" human being: Instead of having a human soul like the rest of us, Jesus' soul was mysteriously "replaced" by the eternal Word. Once again the point is clear: God doesn't *really* want to associate intimately with human beings.

The shift in emphasis represented by Eudoxius' statement serves as a good introduction to the next round of argument between Church thinkers. An important transition point has now been reached in the Church's thinking, although the open hostility among the bishops may at first obscure the fact that the *focus* of the debate had shifted. If anything, the episcopal factions which arise during the next theological storm are even more bellicose than their predecessors.

As we leave behind us the Trinitarian speculation of the third and fourth centuries, we enter into a most difficult area of Christian thought. In comparison, the Trinitarian debate we have just concluded is perfectly easy to follow! At least there we had our own human intuition into interpersonal relationships as a rough model to follow. The Christological debate, on the other hand, is grounded almost entirely in abstract speculation and grows out of an ancient view of psychology which most of us find difficult to understand. So, if you can make it through this chapter and the next, you've got early Church history made.

As we enter this Christological fracas we should not worry that our brains have suddenly become sluggish. It is doubtful that even the original Christological writers really understood each other. Yet these discussions have far-reaching importance. There are still wide differences of belief among Christians today over the relationship between Christ's divine and human natures. These differences can be traced to the very period we are about to study.

The question to keep uppermost as we begin the Christological controversy is this: What does the incarnation mean to *me*? Has my humanity been radically transformed into something godlike, or am I just so much matter and energy? In actuality this is *the* question for the 20th century. Are we humans little sparks of God, or are we robots to be manipulated for someone else's pleasure?

TWO VIEWS ON THE INCARNATION

As early as the third century Christian thinkers had addressed themselves to the question of the divine-human union in the person of Jesus. But only in the mid-fourth century did it became essential for the Church to come to a definitive understanding of this union. Nicene theologians gradually came to see that Trinitarian speculation had tremendous implications for Christology.

As Athanasius asked, "How is it possible for someone not to err with regard to the Son's incarnate presence if he is altogether ignorant of the genuine and true generation of the Son from the Father?"[2] Yet, the first Catholic thinkers to tackle the Christological issue possessed neither the insight nor the terminology to prevent future controversy. Two schools of thought gradually developed on the question of Christology.

'Logos-Flesh' Christology

The first school of thought, *logos-flesh* Christology, supported the idea that the eternal Word was united only to Jesus' flesh (or body), and not to his entire person—body and *soul* (which for the ancients was somewhat similar to our concept of *mind*). Thus Jesus was believed to be "a man in whom God's mind operated." And since the mind was the seat of all thinking and feeling, proponents of this school of Christology said, for example, that *God* got hungry and tired. Attributing Christ's human characteristics to God in this way was known as the *communicatio idiomatum*, or "communication of properties."

This doctrine stressed that whatever one said of Christ's *human* nature could be said also of his *divine* nature. Thus it is perfectly proper, as Athanasius himself said, to call Mary the "Mother of God" (*Theotokos* in Greek). For Athanasius, once the eternal Word united with Jesus' body, it was accurate to say that Christ's flesh had *become* "God's body." The body, as it were, got absorbed into the all-encompassing reality of God's mind. Advocates of *logos-flesh* Christology tended, therefore, to focus exclusively on Christ's divinity.

Some of the more extreme advocates of *logos-flesh* Christology were so insistent on preserving the immutability (unchangeableness) of the divine nature in Christ that they taught the impossibility of any real moral development in Christ's life. Such events as Jesus' temptation in the desert were seen merely as allegorical teachings regarding deeper spiritual realities. How could the absolute, unchanging God really be tempted, they asked.

For these extremists Jesus was different from other persons in that he lacked the ordinary spiritual dimension (soul) possessed by all other humans. In place of Jesus' human soul there existed the eternal Word, which "carried" his body, but which was not fully integrated with this body. The Second Person of the Trinity *"bore* flesh,"[3] they said, but did not truly *become* flesh. Jesus, then, was truly God, but not truly man.

The first Christian thinkers to recognize the dangers of this way of thinking were the three Cappadocians (see pp. 75-78). Since they supported the idea of salvation-as-deification, the Cappadocians wondered how humanity's salvation could be accomplished if God had become only *partially* a man. As Gregory of Nazianzus stated their case:

> For that which Christ has not assumed (a human mind) he has not healed; but that which is united in his Godhead is also saved. If only half Adam fell, then that which Christ assumes and saves may be half also; but if the whole of Adam's nature fell, it must be united to the whole nature of him that was begotten, and so be saved as a whole.[4]

In other words, Gregory said, Jesus truly possessed a human soul (mind), and when Jesus saved humanity, he saved and redeemed every aspect of the human person, not just human "flesh." Humanity's most unique characteristic—its ability to think, reason, feel and love—has been made godlike by the incarnation. Once again, the Church expressed its belief in humanity as God's very image.

Because of the Cappadocians' thinking on this subject, extreme *logos-flesh* Christology (known as "Apollinarism," after Bishop Apollinaris of Laodicea) was condemned at the Council of Constantinople in 381 (see reference to this on p. 80). Yet, *logos-flesh* Christology continued to have many adherents, especially in the episcopal see of Alexandria.

'Logos-Man' Christology
Certain Christian thinkers in Antioch didn't care for the

Alexandrians' continuing flirtation with *logos-flesh* Christology. To the Antiochenes, the Alexandrians were "pie-in-the-sky" Platonists trying to hide their disgust for the idea of God-become-man under a smoke screen of lofty philosophizing. The Antiochenes felt themselves to be more down-to-earth and realistic on the subject of the incarnation. The school of Antioch gradually emerged, therefore, as the opponent of Alexandrian Christology. (While it is somewhat artificial to draw a clear distinction between Antioch and Alexandria here, this division will nonetheless serve as a useful organizational tool in the pages ahead.)

In opposition to the Alexandrian/*logos-flesh* Christology, the Antiochene thinkers developed what is known as *logos-man* Christology. They believed that the divine Word was united to a *man*, not just to "flesh." Extreme advocates of this school of thought tended to go to the opposite extreme from the Alexandrians by overemphasizing Christ's *similarity* to human beings with less stress on his divinity.

Contrary to the *logos-flesh* school, the *logos-man* theologians did not attribute Christ's human activities to his divine nature. Thus, for example, *logos-man* thinkers felt it ridiculous to say that God had lived in Galilee or that God got hungry and tired. They especially stressed the importance of Christ's moral development. According to them, Scripture's statement that Jesus "progressed steadily in wisdom and age and grace" (Luke 2:52) was a literal description of Christ's human maturation process.

This example illustrates the two schools' different starting points. The *logos-flesh* school tended to interpret Scripture allegorically, while the *logos-man* theologians approached the Bible from a historical perspective, and took it literally. One Antiochene theologian, for example, thought it improper to read Scripture without following closely a given passage's "occasion and historical connection."[5]

The Alexandrians interpreted the Bible so as to make it consistent with the *communicatio idiomatum* doctrine which attributed Jesus' human actions to his divinity. The Alexandrians saw the greatest confirmation of this doctrine in the Gospels' miracle stories. Surely, they believed, more than Jesus' humanity had been involved in the miracles. Pope Leo the Great, a supporter of the *communicatio idiomatum*, wrote, "To walk on the back of the sea with feet that do not sink and to still the rising of the waves by rebuking the wind—this is unambiguously divine."[6]

The Antiochene theologians, on the other hand, had no difficulty in attributing Jesus' miracles to his humanity. If it was *God* who walked on the water then, in their view, no real miracle had been performed. When Jesus the *man* walked on water, however, it is accurate to say that a true miracle occurred.

One of the founders of the *logos-man* school was Theodore of Mopsuestia (c. 350-428). In order to stress the importance of Christ's humanity, Theodore used rather troubling language. "What possible resemblance," he asked, "can exist between two things so widely separated from each other *as Christ's divine and human natures*?"[7] The word *nature* became very important to the debate. Theodore and the Antiochene theologians insisted that Christ had two natures—a human and a divine nature. Many of the Alexandrians said Christ had only one nature; as they put it, "the one nature of God the Word incarnate."

With these two poles of thought trying to define the divine-human union in Christ, no common doctrinal solution could be reached. On the one hand, the Alexandrian/*logos-flesh* position tended to negate Christ's humanity. On the other, the Antiochene/*logos-man* teaching cast doubt on the divinity of the man Jesus.

The Heart of the Matter

Here we reach the very heart of the early Church's continuing attempt to understand the incarnation. Unless the Church could creatively resolve the dichotomy between the extremists on both sides of this question, the incarnation could really be said to be pointless.

If, as some Alexandrians would have it, Jesus was "all God," then what real significance does Jesus' life have for me? How can this supreme divinity really relate to my human sufferings, doubts and problems if he really didn't possess my human reasoning and emotions?

But if, as some Antiochenes would have it, Jesus was not of fully divine nature, why should I devote my life to him any more than I should to any other noble man in whom divinity somehow manifested itself? Why is Jesus different from Buddha, Gandhi or any of today's enlightened gurus and masters?

The conflict between the two positions was resolved, oddly enough, during the course of a knock-down, drag-out brawl which erupted between the two leading bishops of the Eastern Church: Cyril of Alexandria and Nestorius of Constantinople. For anyone who cherishes the romantic fantasy that bishops are not fallible sinners like everyone else, the story of Cyril and Nestorius should provide a shocking dose of reality. For anyone who pictures the great Church councils as serene assemblies of wise and patient elders conducting their discussion in an aura of celestial peace, the story of the Council of Ephesus should likewise serve as a brusque revelation. Let's take up that story at its origin.

CYRIL AND NESTORIUS

Cyril became Bishop of Alexandria in 412 and occupied this episcopal office until 444. Second only to Athanasius', his was the longest and most influential tenure of any Alexandrian bishop. One of the most shameful incidents in the history of the early Church occurred during his episcopacy. A learned female philosopher named Hypatia, the brightest scholar in the Alexandrian Neoplatonic Academy, was murdered by a mob of Christians who—some observers alleged—followed the orders of Cyril himself. Hypatia's major crime was that she dared to be a brilliant woman in a city where much of the Christian hierarchy was misogynistic.

Whatever his personal failings, Cyril was nonetheless a creative and original theologian. Although an Alexandrian, he skillfully avoided the more extreme conclusions of the *logos-flesh* position. Following Athanasius and the Cappadocians, he developed and systematized the classical Alexandrian teaching on the Trinity and the person of Christ with a precision and clarity previously lacking. We'll get to Cyril's theology shortly, but first we must discuss the background to his famous feud with Bishop Nestorius of Constantinople.

About the year 430, Nestorius's chaplain Anastasius began preaching in Constantinople against the title "Mother of God" (*Theotokos*) as applied to the Virgin Mary. Such usage, he contended, contradicted the fact that Mary had been mother only of the man Jesus. Nestorius supported Anastasius by decreeing that in Constantinople Mary would henceforth be called "Mother of Christ."

Nestorius had studied in Antioch under Theodore of Mopsuestia where he no doubt acquired the Antiochene preference for *logos-man* Christology. Appointed Bishop of Constantinople in 428, Nestorius, like Cyril in Alexandria, embarked on a program to eliminate all traces of heresy and erroneous doctrine from his diocese. When he opposed the *Theotokos*, however, Nestorius ran into stiff opposition from his flock, who from many years past had accepted *Theotokos* as the orthodox title for Mary. Here was a situation where Christian thinking came squarely into conflict with the belief of "ordinary Christians." The Christians of Constantinople virtually revolted against their bishop who was trying to take away from them one of their most cherished beliefs.

When Cyril in Alexandria learned of the controversy raging in Constantinople, he immediately seized the opportunity to advance the causes of Alexandrian theology, Alexandrian prestige and his own political interests. Since he had the full support of the laity and most of the clergy in Constantinople, Cyril's task was an easy one.

In the first of three condescending and arrogant letters to Nestorius, Cyril asked his brother bishop for an explanation of the reports coming to him from Constantinople. Nestorious wrote back an equally nasty reply telling Cyril to mind his own business. Thus began a propaganda war calculated to establish each bishop's respective theological position as orthodox and his opponent's as heretical. In the process, each bishop also engaged in calumnies directed against the other's personal character.

The dispute grew to alarming proportions. Emperor Theodosius II (401-450) watched his capital torn by strife between his subjects and Nestorius, his own handpicked bishop. (Notice how avidly the Eastern Christians followed theological debates.)

Theodosius invited the Eastern metropolitans (chief bishops of a province), the pope and a few other Western bishops to a general council to be convened at Ephesus on Pentecost Sunday, 431. The pope declined the invitation, but appointed Cyril as his representative. Thus the West (through Cyril) and the Alexandrian bishops formed a united front against Nestorius, whose principal allies were the Syrian bishops and their leader, Bishop John of Antioch. Aside from the personality conflicts and political animosity which separated the Western/Alexandrian coalition from the Antiochene/Nestorian faction, the true nature of the controversy was not perfectly clear to all the bishops who came to Ephesus.

The greatest theologian at the Council of Ephesus was undoubtedly Cyril himself. Aside from his desire to humiliate Nestorius, Cyril had a sincere interest in preserving what he considered to be orthodox doctrine. His special contribution was to devise an expression of the divine-human union which avoided the previous extremes of *logos-flesh* Christology.

Cyril's theological position is represented by such statements as the following: "I say that it is appropriate neither for the logos of God apart from humanity (the preexistent Word), nor for the temple born of the woman [Jesus] not united to the logos, to be called Christ Jesus."[8] Nestorius's Christology differed from Cyril's as illustrated by his statement: "the temple [Jesus] created by the Holy Spirit is one, and the God who hallows the temple (the divine Word) is another."[9]

Cyril's position came to be known as the doctrine of the *hypostatic union*, which means that in the one *hypostasis* (used by Cyril to mean "person") of Jesus Christ a human and a divine nature are inseparably joined together. (As we shall see in the next chapter, Cyril's doctrine of the *hypostatic union*, as slightly reformulated by Pope Leo the Great, became official teaching at the Council of Chalcedon in 451.)

In teaching classes on early Church history I have developed this homely explanation of *logos-flesh* Christology, *logos-man* Christology and Cyril's *hypostatic union*: For *logos-flesh* Christology, imagine that my right hand is lying flat on a table. Attached to my right hand is a bar of iron ("humanity"). My left hand holds a powerful magnet ("divinity") and, at the appropriate moment ("the incarnation"), draws my right hand up to itself, virtually "absorbing" my right hand in the process.

In *logos-man* Christology, my left hand ("divinity") is lying on top of my right hand ("humanity"), which has a tiny spring coiled beneath it. At the appropriate moment ("incarnation"), the coiled spring releases and my right hand *pushes* my left hand upwards (to "heaven"), almost completely on the right hand's own power.

The *hypostatic union* model is much simpler. At the moment of the incarnation my two hands clasp together, fingers intertwined, and both hands simultaneously *lift each other* upwards. Each hand is still a hand. Neither loses its identity. But in the grasp both hands have upon each other something entirely new and unique takes place; as Cyril put it, two "natures" (human and divine) inseparably unite to form one person (Jesus Christ). This inseparable union of two natures in one person forms "something new"—the Word made flesh—and it is this "something new" which distinguishes the Christian incarnation from all other religions' teachings on divinity manifested in humanity. As one modern theologian has put it, "Being a Christian has always meant the indissoluble binding together of God and the human person."[10]

At the Council of Ephesus the Church struggled to define this understanding of the incarnation as normative Catholic doctrine, but because of the personal and ecclesiastical intrigues which dominated the council, the Church achieved only a partial success.

THE COUNCIL OF EPHESUS

When Cyril arrived in Ephesus he quickly took charge of the proceedings. In opposition to 68 bishops and the emperor's own legate, Cyril connived to select the date on which the council was to begin its work. He deliberately chose a date which made it impossible for Bishop John and his Antiochene bishops to arrive on time. Nestorius boycotted the council's opening altogether, on the grounds that not all bishops were in attendance. Together with some 150 bishops, Cyril moved ahead with Nestorius's condemnation.

Cyril's theology was approved by the council, while Nestorius's was condemned. Nestorius was deposed as a bishop, and in a formal letter to the "new Judas," the majority bishops notified Nestorius of their decree of excommunication.

When Bishop John of Antioch and his colleagues finally arrived in Ephesus four days later, they quickly convened a counter-synod of some 50 bishops, and voted to depose Cyril. The emperor intervened by invalidating the decisions of both assemblies and by deposing and arresting both Cyril and Nestorius. Cyril spent huge sums of money to win the emperor's staff to his position, and eventually bribed his jailer to release him from confinement by promising the man a handsome ecclesiastical post in Alexandria.

One may ask at this point whether the "Council" of Ephesus really achieved anything lasting. In spite of the bishops' decidedly unchristian behavior, the council did achieve several theological breakthroughs. By approving Cyril's theology the majority party declared the doctrine of the *communicatio idiomatum* and Mary's title as Mother of God (*Theotokos*) to be expressive of normative Christianity. The minority party led by John of Antioch, although not communicating with the majority, also made a significant contribution at Ephesus. While not abandoning their insistence on two separate natures in Christ, the Antiochenes passed a resolution supporting a Christology of "one Christ, one Son, one Lord" in which—because of a *union of natures*—Mary could properly be called *Theotokos*. The minority on its own initiative thus moved close to the *hypostatic union* theology, thereby abandoning Nestorius—who now stood virtually alone. They also opened the way for a later compromise with the Alexandrians (which we will discuss in the next chapter).

If John of Antioch and his Syrian bishops had simply communicated with Cyril and his supporters, the two groups probably could have worked out a compromise formula which would have satisfied everyone. Instead, the two groups nervously suspected each other of promoting heresy. Cyril, in particular, simply lumped all the Syrian bishops together as heretical "Nestorians," when such a characterization was in fact incorrect.

At Ephesus it was Cyril's *interpretation* of Nestorius's theology which prevailed, and thus it may have been simply Cyril's gloss, rather than Nestorius's actual beliefs, which were condemned by the majority party. In the heat of battle, Nestorius had painted himself into a corner by using exaggerated language. To combat Cyril's doctrine of the *hypostatic union*, Nestorius spoke in terms of a "conjunction" of two natures, which he defined as a "union of will" rather than a true physical union. Nestorius sealed his own fate by refusing to compromise on the *Theotokos*, a decision which forced him to deny one of the Church's oldest and most deeply held beliefs.

Notice that the Council of Ephesus formulated no new Creed. The climate at Ephesus was too stormy for Creed-making. What happened at Ephesus was a warlike confrontation between two belligerent camps which, in spite of their human jealousy and suspicion, managed to issue "position papers" (as we would call them today) which in 20 years would give rise to a definitive formulation of the *hypostatic union*. Let's take up this story as we move now from Ephesus to Chalcedon.

CHAPTER SEVEN

'ONE PERSON IN TWO NATURES'

Toward Chalcedon and Two Eastern Churches

T he Council of Ephesus did not resolve the Christological issues for long. This chapter chronicles several more episodes in that debate leading to a new Creed at the Council of Chalcedon. But despite the Church's continuing struggle to define the incarnation satisfactorily, some Christians were still unable to accept the most fundamental truth of revelation—that God truly became a human being. Thus, in the aftermath of the Council of Chalcedon, some Eastern Christians of the extreme *logos-flesh* persuasion, the Monophysites, left the Catholic Church. For these Christians, rational speculation was never able to reconcile with revelation.

Through the involvement of a theologian-pope at Chalcedon, the West now entered into the Eastern Christological fracas and helped to resolve it. In the next chapter we will pick up again on the development of the Western Church. But that gets ahead of our story.

THE AFTERMATH OF EPHESUS

Both sides came away from the Council of Ephesus nursing feelings of resentment, suspicion and frustration. When the dust of the council had settled, several bishops began to seek means of reconciling the rival factions and bringing about a more charitable resolution of their theological differences. The emperor, too, moved to heal the wounds which the council had opened.

The Formula of Union (433)

Emperor Theodosius appointed Bishop Acacius of Berea—a man considered to be nonpartisan and saintly by both sides—to look into the possibility of reconciling the Alexandrians and the Antiochenes. The Antiochenes were the first to budge. Prompted by Bishop Acacius, Bishop John of Antioch wrote to Cyril that he accepted the *Theotokos* as an expression of orthodoxy, and that he agreed to the deposition of Nestorius. Cyril, turning uncharacteristically conciliatory, accepted the olive branch and replied to John that the two parties now accepted the same belief.

Bishop Theodoret of Cyrrhus (c. 393-466), the leading Antiochene theologian and a friend of Nestorius himself, drew up a compromise document known as the Formula of Union (433). The Formula declared Christ to be "perfect God and perfect man consisting of rational soul and body, of one substance with us in his manhood, so that there is a *union of two natures*; on which ground we confess Christ to be one, and Mary to be mother of God" (emphasis added).[1] Although they could not have known it at the time, the bishops who signed the Formula of Union were witnesses to the last working compromise on this issue in the history of the early Church.

With Cyril's death events were set in motion leading to the entrenchment of bitterly hostile Christological camps which have opposed each other to the present day. The accompanying chart of unfolding events enables us to follow better the upcoming "plot."

The Attempt to Overthrow the Formula of Union

	Alexandria	Antioch	Constantinople
1)	Cyril is succeeded as bishop by Dioscorus. Dioscorus wants to move away from the "two-nature" formula, back to the more extreme *logos-flesh* Christology.	John is succeeded as bishop by Domnus. Theodoret of Cyrrhus is the real "power behind the throne." (Theodoret had drawn up the Formula of Union.)	Nestorius is eventually succeeded as bishop by Flavian, who supported the Formula of 433 (i.e., "two-nature" Christology).
2)	Dioscorus for deceitful reasons supports Eutyches, a monk in Constantinople who wants to go back to extreme *logos-flesh* Christology.	Theodoret and the Antiochenes are "set up" and condemned as heretics by Dioscorus.	Eutyches the monk teaches a "one-nature" Christology. His views are condemned at a Synod in 448.
3)	Dioscorus controls the	Domnus and Theodoret	Emperor Theodosius II

| Synod of 449 in order to rehabilitate Eutyches, condemn the Antiochenes and Flavian, and reestablish Alexandrian "one-nature" Christology. | are deposed, and the Formula of Union of 433 is repudiated at the Synod of 449. | convenes a Synod in 449—"The Robbers' Synod." Bishop Flavian is deposed. |

Political Sidetracks

Having observed the bishops' unchristian behavior at Ephesus, it should come as no surprise that petty jealousies and ecclesiastical rivalries become as important to the flow of early Christian thinking as the theological issues. Let's look at one example of how personality differences and ecclesiastical ambition sidetracked the Church from its attempt to achieve a universally acceptable formula on Christ's divine-human union.

As the chart shows, John was succeeded as bishop of Antioch by his nephew Domnus, while Alexandria's new bishop was a man named Dioscorus. Dioscorus (444-454) was assertive, energetic and scheming; Domnus was sluggish, vacillating and timid. Bishop Domnus of Antioch, as if acknowledging his own ineptness, turned over control of his see to Bishop Theodoret of Cyrrhus.

Dioscorus adamantly opposed the Formula of Union and immediately sought for a way to annul it. His motives were twofold: (1) He advocated the extreme *logos-flesh* Christology which tended to ignore Christ's humanity. (2) He wanted to assert himself as the most influential bishop of the Eastern Church.

Dioscorus seemed to have inherited all of Cyril's bad qualities and none of the good. Two years after Dioscorus became Bishop of Alexandria, Flavian (446-449) was named bishop of the third major see of the Eastern Church (Constantinople). Flavian supported the Formula of Union but did not have the political savvy to withstand Dioscorus's machinations against the Antiochenes.

Dioscorus soon found a way to disrupt the tentative reconciliation that Cyril and John had earlier achieved through the Formula of Union. A monk living in Constantinople named Eutyches provided the opportunity.

Eutyches was a man of great pretension and little intelligence who thought he had struck upon the perfect Christological formula. He taught that, although there had been *two* natures *before* the union in Christ there was only *one* nature *after* the union. Eutyches's teaching appealed to Dioscorus because it served as a convenient vehicle by which to reinstate the Christological controversy.

Dioscorus's plan was to (underhandedly) have Eutyches condemned as a heretic by a synod of bishops. Diocorus could then publicly come to the monk's assistance and emerge as the new champion of the old *logos-flesh* Christology. He hoped to stir up enough controversy with the Antiochenes to bring the old quarrel out into the open again.

Dioscorus's scheme worked perfectly. At a synod in Constantinople in 448—after Dioscorus had privately instructed the emperor's legate to vote against Eutyches—the monk was predictably condemned.

Dioscorus at once rejected the synod's decision and made a great show of offering refuge and support to the "brutally maligned" Eutyches. Then, counting on Alexandria's old alliance with Rome, Dioscorus encouraged Eutyches to appeal to Pope Leo. Bishop Flavian, president of the synod which had condemned Eutyches, sent Leo the transcript of Eutyches's synodal testimony.

Leo—contrary to what Dioscorus had expected—immediately declared Eutyches to be a heretic. This caused a substantial ruckus in the East, and prompted the emperor to call for a new council of bishops to meet in 449. The emperor's decision played right into Dioscorus's hands. Dioscorus saw the new council as the opportunity to secure official repudiation of the Formula of Union of 433 and the Christological presuppositions behind it.

Ephesus II: 'The Robbers' Synod'

The emperor invited Pope Leo to the council—which also met in Ephesus—but Leo declined to come in person. Instead, he sent three representatives who brought with them the pope's *Dogmatic Letter to Flavian*, in which Leo set forth his Christological position. Before we look at Leo's *Tome*, as the letter came to be called, let's follow the events of "Ephesus Council II" to their sad conclusion.

The emperor appointed Dioscorus to preside at the council. The council rapidly came to resemble an armed camp rather than a religious assembly. The emperor surrounded the church in which the bishops met (the same church used for "Ephesus I" in 431) with armed guards; Eutyches brought along a throng of bellicose monks; and Dioscorus surrounded himself with Alexandrian bodyguards.

When the pope's representatives from Rome stood to read Leo's *Tome*, Dioscorus's agents shouted them down. When the pope's Eastern supporter, Bishop Eusebius of Dorylaeum, tried to speak, Dioscorus's supporters likewise drove Eusebius from the floor. A majority of the 140 bishops in attendance then approved a decree reinstating Eutyches and deposing Bishops Flavian and Eusebius. When the minority protested, Dioscorus called in a raging mob from outside the church which bullied the recalcitrant bishops into signing the decree.

Bishop Flavian died a few days later, perhaps because of the threats which he had suffered at the hands of Dioscorus's thugs. At a later session of the council, Dioscorus completed his victory by procuring the denunciation of the chief architect of the Formula of Union, Theodoret of Cyrrhus, and his two principal supporters, Bishops Domnus of Antioch and Ibas of Edessa.

This "Robbers' Synod," as Pope Leo later called it, did much more than simply reinstate the old *logos-flesh* Christology. Rather, Ephesus II established a *hyper-extension* of *logos-flesh* Christology—a doctrine which came to be known as the *Monophysite* heresy (from the Greek for "one nature").

In Cyril's day the Alexandrian school had often expressed itself in terms of two natures "mixed" together in one divine-human union. Yet it nonetheless had recognized Christ's *two* natures. Now, spurred on by the fanatical Dioscorus, more extreme elements in the Alexandrian camp felt confident to assert unambiguously at Ephesus II that Christ possessed only one nature—a divine nature which had fully absorbed his human nature. Momentarily at least, the Eastern Church had retreated squarely into *Monophysitism*.

Western Theology Enters the Debate

Pope Leo the Great (pope from 440-461) was the first Bishop of Rome to be a significant theologian in his own right. A representative of the Western theological tradition, his Christology drew upon the work of Tertullian and Augustine. (We discussed Tertullian on pp. 31-33, and will discuss Augustine in Chapter Nine.)

Tertullian had long before written of "two substances" in the one person of Christ, bound together in such a way that Jesus possessed a human soul. Augustine later developed Tertullian's thought down to Leo's time. By Ephesus I (431) the West had come to accept a Christology of "two natures in one person" as an expression of normative Christian belief. Thus when Leo, then a deacon, first learned of Nestorius's views, he became a staunch advocate of Alexandrian Christology and a supporter of Cyril.

As Leo continued to follow the debate in the East in the years after Ephesus I, he became aware of the dangers involved in extending the Alexandrian position to its limits. At the same time, he came to see the merits of the Antiochene viewpoint. Relying on the work of Western theologians who had gone before him, he began to work out what amounted to a synthesis of the Alexandrian and Antiochene positions.

Leo's starting point was Christ's work of salvation, what Leo called a "wonderful exchange," by which Christ "entered into a bargain of salvation, taking upon himself what was ours (sin), and granting us what was his (Sonship)."[2] In Leo's approach the distinction between Christ's two natures was preserved—in harmony with Antiochene Christology—while at the same time the *immutability* (unchangeableness) of Christ's divinity was upheld—in sympathy with Alexandrian Christology.

Leo wrote that in Christ "each *form* does the acts which are appropriate to it, in communion with the other; the Logos, that is, performing what is appropriate to it, and the flesh carrying out what is appropriate to the flesh."[3] For this reason Leo had no difficulty in saying that the Lord of glory had suffered and that Mary had been Mother of God.

This sounds much like pure Alexandrian/*logos-flesh* Christology. Yet as Leo got involved in the controversy over Eutyches, he showed how his position affirmed the *distinction* between Christ's two natures as professed by the Antiochenes.

Leo wrote that Eutyches's error had been to deny Christ's oneness with humanity. In his *Tome* Leo wrote, "For, as God is not changed by the showing of pity, so the man (Jesus) is not swallowed up by the dignity (of the incarnation)."[4] Leo rejected Eutyches's use of "one nature after the union" because in this formula he saw a return to the error condemned at Constantinople in 381 that Christ's human nature had been absorbed into his divine nature.

After Ephesus II ("The Robbers' Synod"), Leo immediately began to urge Emperor Theodosius to reverse that synod's decisions. Theodosius rebuffed Leo, but in July of 450 Theodosius died. His sister Pulcheria and her husband Marcian, the new imperial couple, immediately set about to undo the work of "The Robbers' Synod." They restored exiled Antiochene bishops to their sees and called for another general council. At this new council the Christological synthesis of Leo (the Bishop of Rome) would replace the Monophysite Christology of Dioscorus (the Bishop of Alexandria).

The Council of Chalcedon

On October 8, 451, in Chalcedon, located across the Bosporus from Constantinople, over 500 bishops came together for the Fourth Ecumenical Council. (It would be accurate to consider this the "first" truly ecumenical council, since for the first time the Western position as well as the Eastern was formally advanced.) When Leo's delegates successfully prohibited Dioscorus from taking a seat at the council, it became immediately evident to all that new forces had taken control of the conciliar leadership.

Chalcedon was not to be another kangaroo court such as the Robbers' Synod had been. Bishops who had sided with Dioscorus at Ephesus II publicly repented and asked their brothers for forgiveness. Dioscorus himself was excommunicated and banished. Flavian (posthumously) and Theodoret of Cyrrhus were restored to the Church's communion, and Eutyches was formally condemned as a heretic.

With these disciplinary matters attended to, the bishops turned to the theological issues.

At the direction of the emperor a committee of 23 bishops was selected to draft a new Creed directed specifically to the Christological issues we have been discussing in this chapter and the last. At the urging of the emperor, the bishops approved the new statement of orthodoxy, which read as follows:

> *Following then, the holy Fathers,* we all with one voice teach that it should be confessed that our Lord Jesus Christ is one and the same God, the Same perfect in Godhead, the Same perfect in manhood, truly God and truly man, the Same (consisting) of a rational soul and a body; *homoousios* with the Father as to his Godhead, and the Same *homoousios* with us as to his manhood; in all things like unto us, sin only excepted; begotten of the Father before ages as to his Godhead, and in the last days, the Same, for us and for our salvation, of Mary the Virgin *Theotokos* as to his manhood;

> One and the same Christ, Son, Lord, Only begotten, made known *in two natures* [which exist] without confusion, without change, without division, without separation; the difference of the natures having been in no wise taken away by reason of the union, but rather the properties of each being preserved, and [both] concurring into one Person (*prosopon*) and one *hypostasis*—not parted or divided into two persons (*prosopa*), but one and the same Son and Only-begotten, the divine Logos, the Lord Jesus Christ; even as the prophets from of old [have spoken] concerning him, and as the Lord Jesus Christ himself has taught us, and as the *Symbol of the Fathers* has delivered to us[5] (emphasis added).

The new Creed has several significant points. Notice that the bishops see themselves as "following the holy fathers." The Church now consciously aligns itself with the traditional teaching of the earliest Christian thinkers. The teaching of these "fathers" had come to be thought of as an unerring criterion of orthodoxy.

Notice also that the first paragraph closely follows Nicene theology. Jesus is called "truly God and truly man," *homoousios* with both the Father and humanity. His eternal preexistence is emphasized by the phrase "begotten of the Father before ages as to his Godhead." Then the *communicatio idiomatum* is upheld as the bishops formally acknowledge Mary to be the Mother of God.

In the second paragraph the Creed follows Pope Leo's teaching of "*in* two natures." It specifically rejects Monophysite Christology by affirming that Christ's two natures exist "without confusion, without change, without division, without separation."

The bishops at Chalcedon close with the words, "as the symbol [remember that "symbol" meant "creed"] of the Fathers has delivered to us." Thus the Nicene-Constantinopolitan Creed is itself established as a criterion of orthodoxy on a par with Scripture (that is, "the prophets," "the Lord Jesus himself").

With the Council of Chalcedon the Church reestablished its three ancient criteria of orthodoxy: (1) Apostolicity, as contained in the fathers' teaching, (2) Scripture and (3) Creed. Through all the long and tortuous intellectual debates leading to the Creed of Chalcedon, in the end the bishops had not departed from the three norms of orthodoxy established as early as the second century: the teaching of the Apostles, the canon of Scripture and the ancient rules of faith.

While the Creed of Chalcedon was a great triumph for Christian thinking, it was also a victory for Christian belief. The faith of the "little people" still inspired and guided the bishops at Chalcedon in 451 as it had at Nicaea in 325 and at Constantinople in 381. The belief of the Christian people as expressed in their ancient rules of faith was always the point beyond which Christian orthodoxy never desired to go.

Pope Leo the Great's Victory: A New Synthesis

The Chalcedonian Creed, aside from achieving a synthesis of faith and reason as the Creeds of Nicaea and Constantinople had done, brought together the best of Alexandrian, Antiochene and Nicene theology. And since it was Pope Leo's *Tome* which inspired this synthesis, the Creed of Chalcedon can really be seen as a doctrinal victory for Leo, the papacy and the West. (The development of the papacy will be taken up in the next chapter.) It was not idle flattery when the bishops at Chalcedon proclaimed that in Leo's *Tome*, "Peter had spoken."

After the Council of Chalcedon (as after Nicaea, Ephesus and Constantinople), there were those who refused to accept the majority's decision. The Chalcedon dissenters were the new Monophysite party—those who adhered to the extreme version of the old *logos-flesh* Christology. The Monophysites wanted nothing to do with Chalcedon's "two-nature" Jesus; the "two-nature" formula made Jesus too human and too little divine.

When the pro-Chalcedon Emperor Marcian died in 457, these Monophysite zealots vented their hostility against the new Creed of Chalcedon. In Alexandria, as a sign of worse things to come, the pro-Chalcedon bishop was murdered by a Monophysite mob. An anonymous Monophysite monk summed up the vehemence of the anti-Chalcedon sentiment when he wrote, "Anathema to the unclean Synod of Chalcedon! Anathema to everyone who agrees with it!"[6]

THE MONOPHYSITE CONTROVERSY

The Monophysite party concluded that Chalcedon had not gone far enough in emphasizing the divine element in Christ's divine-human union. They believed the bishops at Chalcedon had perverted the unquestionably orthodox formula—that Christ was *homoousios* with the *Father*—by equating this relationship between Father and Son to the Son's relationship to *humanity*.

If Jesus Christ were truly *homoousios* with the Father, Monophysites said, then he should—as truly God—be incorruptible, omniscient and uncreated. Accordingly, some Monophysites taught that Christ's body was incorruptible from the moment of incarnation rather than from his resurrection, that he had known all things perfectly at all times, and that he came into being not as a created man but as the spontaneous expression of God's own eternal existence. Notice how *un*human the Monophysites wanted to make Jesus.

This extreme Monophysitism was eventually defeated by both political and theological counterattack. But that struggle gravely eroded the status of the Creed of Chalcedon as an acceptable formula of orthodoxy in the Eastern Church. (The Monophysites posed no danger in the West where Christians, even before Chalcedon, had been long accustomed to the "one-person, two-nature" formula.)

The opposition to Chalcedon was centered in Egypt. (To this day the majority Christian party in Egypt is the Coptic Church—whose members are direct descendants of the fifth-century Egyptian Monophysites.) The Monophysites made great inroads in Palestine and Syria as well, oftentimes supported by violent mobs who drove pro-Chalcedon bishops from their sees.

Not all of this hostility stemmed from subtle theological debate. Monophysitism provided a means for long-suppressed national minorities to express their contempt for the imperial government, which was closely associated in the popular mind with the Council of

Chalcedon. As the Eastern Empire's own internal political problems grew ever more intense, the Monophysites gained the freedom to form themselves into clusters of national churches scattered throughout the East. Many of these bodies survive to this day.

The Monophysite controversy caused such havoc in the East that it became obvious to all that a new council was needed to reconcile pro-Chalcedonians and Monophysites. But it was also obvious that only a strong emperor could control and direct such a council. The Eastern bishops had become so divided that the Eastern Church was now incapable of healing itself. Into the theological arena stepped an emperor who was both a strong political ruler and a highly skilled theologian.

JUSTINIAN AND THE SECOND COUNCIL OF CONSTANTINOPLE

Justinian (527-565) was the greatest emperor of the "Byzantine East." I do not say "Eastern Roman Empire," because by Justinian's time, it is no longer accurate to think in terms of Western and Eastern sectors of the one Empire. The West had long been ruled by barbarian chieftains rather than by Roman emperors. (We take up the collapse of the Western Empire shortly.) The Byzantine Empire developed its own culture, politics and theology.

Justinian believed that it was his duty to dictate theological policy to the Church. He did this so forcefully that the East developed an understanding of Church-State relations in which the emperor came to be seen as the overseer of Church life. Justinian thus sought to impose his own solution on the Monophysite controversy, but actually alienated the two factions even more.

To settle the controversy Justinian decided to convene a fifth "Ecumenical Council" in Constantinople. The council—in actuality merely an Eastern synod—convened on May 5, 553, with 166 Eastern bishops in attendance. The Council's doctrinal achievement is perhaps best summarized in a turbid formula condemning anyone who professed that "God the Logos who performed miracles was another than Christ who suffered."[7] The *Theotokos* was reaffirmed as Mary's proper title.

The Council of Chalcedon was designated as a "holy Synod," but it was not really clear that Leo's "two-nature" synthesis at Chalcedon had been upheld. The second Council of Constantinople really satisfied neither Chalcedonians nor Monophysites.

Two Separate Eastern Churches

Justinian's successors continued his effort to reconcile Chalcedonians and Monophysites, trying every tactic from appeasement

104

to persecution, with no success. The Byzantine emperors could not understand that there were now two separate Eastern Churches in existence, one which supported the Creed of Chalcedon, and another which regarded itself as irreconcilably opposed to that Creed.

The two factions were never again to be united. A Monophysite bishop named James Bardaeus ("the Beggar," 500-578) traveled in disguise throughout the East ordaining Monophysite priests and bishops, laying the foundation for the Monophysite Church which took James's name. Today these "Jacobites" are found principally in the Syrian Orthodox Church.

The continuing struggle over the Monophysite issue leads us into the medieval period of Eastern Christianity (not covered in this volume). We leave the Eastern Church torn between Monophysites and Chalcedonians, and return to the story of the Western Church as we left it in the fourth century, involved in the Donatist controversy (see p. 55).

As we leave Eastern Christianity we notice that the fundamental questions raised by the Christian gospel have not yet been answered to everyone's satisfaction: Did God truly join himself to humanity in the most intimate way by becoming fully human? Has humanity truly been ennobled and raised to a new status by God's redeeming touch? Or is humanity still a lesser form of creation, unworthy of anything other than a purely "spiritual" salvation? The Church's continuing efforts to answer these questions reveal not only what humanity believes about God but, more importantly perhaps, what humanity believes about itself.

By the end of the period covered in this book, the Eastern Church had not resolved the tension between two competing views of salvation—one which sees God as "up there," lifting humanity into himself, the other which sees God as inextricably involved in the human struggle, assisting humanity to gain its freedom.

I invite you to examine your own belief. Which of these competing viewpoints expresses what the incarnation means for you?

Reconsider the faith of the earliest believers as expressed in their primitive rules of faith and incorporated into the great syntheses of faith and reason achieved by the bishops at Nicaea (325), Constantinople (381) and Chalcedon (451). Then answer the question, "What does the incarnation mean to *me*?" Or, as Jesus himself once asked his own disciples, "And you, who do *you* say that I am?"

CHAPTER EIGHT

THE WESTERN CHURCH AFTER CONSTANTINE

312 A.D.—600 A.D.: An Overview

During the involved theological debates discussed in the last few chapters, you may have felt like asking, "Why was the Western Church so hesitant to engage in these theological debates?" Or, "Why didn't the pope attend the early councils or intervene more directly to settle these theological disputes?" These are "practical" questions that appeal to our Western concern for organization, law and administration. We will take up some of these "practical" issues now. But in doing so, we cease talking about the great Creeds and their role in early Church history.

For the most part the story of the great Creeds has been an "Eastern" story. Individual Westerners (such as Hosius of Cordoba and Pope Leo the Great, for example) made immense contributions to the development of the Creeds. And of course the rules of faith which were incorporated into the Creeds were products of both Western and Eastern congregations. But, by and large, the Creeds were the Easterners' gift to the Church.

In the next three chapters we will look at the Western contribution to the life of the early Church. We will consider such "practical" questions as the development of the papacy and, "How did we get our present system of dioceses and parishes?" Or, "Why are priests required to be celibate?" We will return to the subject of the Creeds in the final chapter, where we again find a great Creed (one originating in the *West*) serving to unite Christian thought and belief.

CHURCH-STATE RELATIONS: A WESTERN VIEW

Under Constantine Western Christians, like their Eastern counterparts, looked upon the emperor as the Church's divinely appointed protector and the defender of orthodoxy. (We left our discussion of Western Christianity in Chapter Two with Constantine's intervention on the side of Catholic Christianity in the early stages of the Donatist controversy (see p. 55). Yet, as imperial policy began to change—and to vacillate—under the rule of Constantine's descendants, Western bishops developed a theory of Church-State relations markedly different from that of the Easterners.

The change in Westerners' thinking took shape especially under the reign of Emperor Constantius (sole emperor, 350-361). Constantius's attitude was ominously revealed to the Western bishops when he told them bluntly, "What I want must be regarded as canon law."[1] Remember that Constantius was an Arian (see p. 69), and he wanted to convert the Western bishops to the Arian interpretation of the incarnation. Perhaps more importantly, however, Constantius wanted the Western bishops to knuckle under and become pliable supporters of imperial policy, as were most Eastern bishops.

Constantius once hid behind a screen at a Western synod, taking notes on the comments of the bishops in attendance. Such behavior drew vehement protest from Western bishops who let the emperor know in unambiguous terms that he was not to meddle in Church affairs. To put pressure on recalcitrant bishops, however, Constantius availed himself of bribery, intimidation and banishment.

One of the most notable of Constantius's Western exiles was Bishop Hilary of Poitiers (c. 315-367), known as the "Athanasius of the West." While in exile in Phrygia (central Turkey) Hilary studied the Eastern Trinitarian debate at close hand. He wrote a lengthy treatise called *On the Trinity* through which he transmitted to the West the latest Eastern theology. Although Hilary was not an original thinker, he was responsible for introducing the West to the theological concepts and the Trinitarian debates which were becoming prominent in the East. One Western thinker influenced by Hilary was Ambrose of Milan (c. 339-397).

Ambrose of Milan

Although he was only a catechumen, in 374 Ambrose was selected by the people of Milan to become their bishop. He was baptized and ordained their bishop in ceremonies separated only by a few days.

Bishop Ambrose at once became a spokesman for ecclesiastical independence. He pointed Western Church-State relations in the exact opposite direction of the approach taken in the East. Resisting Emperor Valentinian's attempt to turn two Catholic basilicas into Arian churches, Ambrose wrote, "To the emperor belong the palaces, to the bishop the churches. You have been entrusted with jurisdiction over public buildings but not over sacred ones....Do not burden yourself with the idea that you have any right as emperor over the things of God."[2] Ambrose's view of Church-State relations was summarized in his famous dictum, "The emperor is in the Church, not *over* the Church."[3]

Ambrose's concern to establish the Church's autonomy vis-a-vis the State is likewise seen in his concern for social justice. He asserted the Church's right to hold the State accountable for upholding the gospel. "We are bound by the law of nature to act for the good of all."[4] Elsewhere he wrote, "The world was created for all in general, yet a handful of the rich endeavor to make it their own preserve."[5]

It was characteristic of Western thinkers to concern themselves as much with Christians' duties in the here-and-now as with their life in the hereafter. Ambrose's contemporary, Jerome, instructed his readers "to clothe Christ in the poor, to visit him in the sick, to feed him in the hungry, to shelter him in the homeless...."[6] And Augustine paved the way for a fully developed theology of social justice in the West when he taught,

> Seek only what God has given you, and from it take only what you need. The superfluities of the rich are the necessities of the poor. When you possess superfluities, you possess the goods of others.[7]

In response to a request by Emperor Gratian (375-383), Ambrose composed a treatise on the Holy Spirit which was largely a paraphrase of Basil the Great's earlier treatise on the subject. Like Hilary, Ambrose contributed significantly to the West's comprehension of the Eastern theological controversies. His writings helped to shape the West's perspective on the *communicatio idiomatum*, and his view of salvation directly affected Pope Leo's *Tome*.

Jerome

The most significant Western thinker before Augustine was an eccentric Italian scholar named Eusebius Hieronymus, known to us as Jerome. If the Church were ever to choose a patron saint for curmudgeons, Jerome would be the unanimous choice. To catch his reader's attention, Jerome was fond of starting his letters with such colorful salutations as, "To So-and-So, not a man but a dog that returns to its own vomit, Greetings!"

Somehow Jerome attracted quite a following of devotees,

particularly among wealthy Italian ladies for whom he no doubt moderated his graphic language. Jerome had been an avid reader of Greek and Roman classics until he started to experience pangs of guilt over the direction in which his study was leading him. The story is told that one Lent he fell ill and suffered a vision in which he heard the Almighty thunder, "You are a Ciceronian, not a Christian!"

From that moment on, Jerome turned his attention to the study of Greek and Hebrew in preparation for his lifelong work, the translation and exegesis of Scripture. His greatest achievement was the *Vulgate*, or translation of the Bible from the original languages into a popular Latin. Jerome's Latin translation of the Bible surpassed previous Latin translations and remained the Catholic Church's standard until recent times.

With the financial assistance of his noble lady-friends, Jerome and his entourage moved to Palestine, where he eventually founded an ascetic community for men in Bethlehem, keeping his female benefactors at a respectable distance for propriety's sake.

From Bethlehem Jerome kept an observant eye on theological happenings throughout East and West, posting scathing denunciations of heresy to the four corners of the Christian world. Jerome joined in the Western effort to chastise the State for its intervention in Church affairs. From his vantage point in the East he had been in a good position to instruct his fellow Westerners on the dangers of imperial domination. "Since the Church has come under Christian emperors," he wrote, "it has indeed grown in power and wealth, but it has decreased in moral strength."[8]

Jerome's correspondents must have trembled to open a letter from him; they never were certain whether he was writing to condemn someone else or themselves. Yet Jerome's scholarship and literary skills always broke through the venomous crust of his writings. When he died Christian thinkers of both East and West felt that the finest mind yet produced in the Western Church had taken leave of them.

THE DEVELOPMENT OF THE PAPACY

Nowhere was the Church's struggle between power and wealth on the one hand and moral strength on the other better illustrated than in the development of the papacy. It was during the fourth century that this institution came of age and began to take shape. Yet as early as the second century the Roman bishops had already begun to construct a doctrine of papal primacy residing in the person of the bishop of Rome.

As the Christian population increased, the need for greater

organization and expansion of the episcopal office grew also. By the second century, one bishop found it impossible to supervise the vast territories of the East with their large numbers of Christians. New bishops had to be ordained. But, as the apostles were not around to ordain these men, the question arose of *priority among bishops*. Who among the bishops stood in sufficient historical linkage with the Apostles to transmit apostolic authority to new bishops?

The Question of Priority

Many Christians thought that only bishops in those cities whose first bishops had themselves been Apostles could ordain and install new bishops. One would have thought, therefore, that the bishop of such cities as Jerusalem and Ephesus would have qualified for such an honor.

Jerusalem, however, was an impractical choice in the early second century because it was plagued by almost constant warfare between Jews and Romans. The church in Ephesus, although tracing its origins to the Apostle Paul, and reputedly pastored at one time by the Apostle John, nonetheless declined in importance as other cities of the Empire outstripped it in *political* significance.

In the end, three local churches claiming apostolic foundation by the Apostle Peter emerged in the second century as the major bishoprics of Christianity: Rome, Antioch and Alexandria. (The latter based its Petrine foundation on the claim that it had been founded by Peter's assistant, Mark.) These three cities (or "sees") became the focal point of apostolic authority in the early Church. New bishoprics were thus founded and new shepherds ordained with the approval of the bishops of these three sees.

Although new bishoprics were "approved," it was still the Christians of local congregations who "elected" their bishops. The bishops of the major three sees would then ratify, as it were, these elections. We will see shortly how the concept of popular election of bishops soon disappeared altogether.

The territories pastored by the early bishops often coincided with the Roman Empire's administrative unit (the *diocese*), and thus these territories came to be known by the same name. (Later, however, the Western usage of *parish* for a subdivision of the diocese was substituted in the East for "diocese" itself. In the East to this day *parish* is often used to define the entire area under a bishop's supervision.)

Rome: Eminent or *Pre*-eminent?

As might be expected, bishops came to have different opinions about the authority of the three major sees, vis-a-vis one another. In the

West, Irenaeus wrote of the Roman Church's preeminent authority to define normative Christianity. Irenaeus called the Roman Church "the greatest and oldest church known to all."[9] In the East, other bishops acknowledged Rome's eminence, but would not have characterized Rome's position as one of *pre*-eminence.

The Roman Church's own claim to preeminent position first becomes evident during the tenure of Bishop Victor (189-198), who asserted a distinct claim to apostlic authority in a controversy with other Churches over the date on which Easter was to be celebrated.

The first significant debate between bishops on the question of Rome's priority was undertaken by Stephen of Rome (254-257) and Cyprian of Carthage (d. 258). Stephen and Cyprian differed on the question of baptism by heretics. Stephen and the Roman Church believed that a Christian baptized in proper form by a heretic did not have to be rebaptized upon converting to Catholic Christianity. Cyprian, on the other hand, stood by the common practice in the North African Church which did require rebaptism.

Stephen urged Cyprian to accept the Roman practice, but Cyprian refused. Stephen died and Cyprian was martyred before the two bishops could settle their disagreement. Their differing views of episcopal authority—Cyprian's collegial and Stephen's hierarchical—were to clash repeatedly during the following centuries of Church history.

Cyprian interpreted Matthew 16:18a ("You are 'Rock,' and on this rock I will build my church") to mean that Christ "is building the church on one man."[10] Yet, Cyprian refines this thought by saying, "The other apostles were all that Peter was, endowed with equal dignity and power, but the start comes from him alone."[11] In a final clarification Cyprian adds, "The episcopate is one, each part of which is held by each one for the whole."[12] Taken together, these three statements indicate that Cyprian saw the *origins* of episcopal authority in Christ's designation of Peter as "rock," but saw the *ongoing exercise* of that authority shared equally by all bishops.

Stephen's understanding of episcopal authority differed from Cyprian's. Stephen believed he was heir to Peter's position as first among the Apostles, and thus as Bishop of Rome he stood first among the bishops. By the end of the early period the West had come to accept Stephen's hierarchical view, while the East favored Cyprian's collegial approach.

Only in the West did the Roman bishop assume sole usage of the title "pope" (from the Greek *pappas* for "father," a title used at first for *all* bishops). The bishops of North Africa, for example, as late as the fifth century called the primate of Carthage "papa," or pope, thus

112

disputing the Roman bishop's sole usage of the title.

The Emperor's Role

When Constantine became sole emperor he respected the prestige of the Roman bishops. Thus Constantine had tried to settle the Donatist controversy through means of a synod headed by the *Roman* Bishop Miltiades (see p. 56). Constantine donated his Lateran Palace to the Roman bishops as their special episcopal residence, and he undertook the construction of the first St. Peter's Basilica. Yet, despite the respect which he accorded to the Roman see, Constantine did not go so far as to consider the Roman bishop first among the other bishops. And, of course, Constantine reserved to himself all major Church decisions.

Under Constantine's sons we first begin to see the Roman bishops asserting the claim of primacy with lasting effect. Pope Julius I (337-352) thought of himself as possessing authority to render binding decisions in both East and West on matters affecting Church discipline. Julius's support for Athanasius (see p. 72), and his opposition to Athanasius' Eastern enemies, went a long way toward advancing the papacy's universalist policies. When Constantius became sole emperor in 350, however, the popes found their efforts to establish Petrine primacy momentarily sidetracked.

Keep in mind that all during this time the Christians in Rome (and Christians in other sees) had been electing their own bishops. Constantius instituted a policy of *appointing* bishops who would carry out his imperial policies. Gradually the Church accepted this procedure, and the practice of popular election of bishops died out. When Constantius died the bishops themselves continued the policy of appointing bishops. One of the last *elected* bishops of Rome was Damasus I (366-384).

It was Damasus who first used the phrase "Apostolic See" in reference to the Roman episcopate. He intended to base Rome's claim to primacy on the Roman Church's foundation by Peter. Eastern sees regarded Damasus' use of the title coolly and retorted that there were several "apostolic sees" within the Church. Undaunted, Damasus continued to advance the cause of papal primacy.

Damasus' successor was Siricius (384-399). According to Jerome, this was an imprudent choice since (also according to Jerome) everyone knew Jerome himself would have been a better choice for the office.

Siricius held the papal office while the influential Ambrose was bishop of Milan, and thus the pope's "primacy" paled into insignificance in comparison to the talents of his famous confrere to the north. The papacy had clearly not developed to the point where a weak pope could surpass in influence a more talented bishop, even in the Italian peninsula where by this time the pope's primacy was taken for granted.

Siricius is important largely for the fact that it was he who developed the concept of the papal *decretal*, a papal letter rendering an authoritative decision on a matter of Church discipline. Like Damasus, Siricius based his authority to render such decisions on his position as successor of the "Rock" on whom Christ founded his Church.

By Siricius' time the papacy, and indeed all of Western society, was experiencing the pressure of a new force in early Church history—the barbarian invasions into the Empire. These invasions greatly affected both the papacy as well as Western and Eastern Church and State.

THE BARBARIAN INVASIONS

The barbarian peoples had settled centuries before Jesus' time in various regions of what is now Germany, France, Scandinavia and the British Isles. Most of the barbarian peoples organized themselves into tribal democracies under an elected chieftain. Generally they were agricultural societies living in accommodation with the Roman power to the south and east. In the mid-fourth century the barbarians' relationship to Rome changed radically when the Huns, a nomadic people from Asia, began to invade the barbarian homelands. Pressured by the Huns, barbarian refugees fled south into the Empire seeking the stability which life in the Empire could provide.

The Roman government reacted poorly to the problems created by the barbarian encroachments, and eventually found itself in a perpetual state of conflict with the largest barbarian tribe, the Visigoths. In 378 when Visigoth horsemen defeated the finest Roman foot soldiers at the Battle of Adrianople, the event signaled the breakdown in the West of the ancient *pax Romana*—the Roman peace which for centuries had maintained order and stability throughout the Empire, and which provided the soil in which the Church had taken root.

Facing a harsh reality, the Western emperors began to assimilate the barbarians into the Roman army and civil service. One of these Romanized barbarians—the Visigoth Alaric—turned on the Romans and invaded Italy, sacking Rome in 410. Alaric's successor, Ataulf, forged a coalition of Visigothic military leadership and Roman civil administration. The Visigoths became, as it were, the Empire's bodyguards, defending the Western half of the Empire from the ravages of other barbarian invaders, such as the Vandals who occupied Spain and

North Africa during Augustine's last days (see p. 134).

Meanwhile, the Huns had formed an alliance with indigenous tribes to the north and began to threaten the Empire in Italy. The Hun chieftain Attila defeated a Roman-Visigothic force and proceeded to march on the city of Rome. Pope Leo I and city officials persuaded Attila to spare the city. When Attila died two years later the Huns' threat withered away, and until 484 the Visigoths continued to dominate the empty shell of imperial government in the West.

In 489 a new tribe known as the Ostrogoths conquered Italy, led by their chieftain, Theodoric the Great. Once in control, Theodoric gained official recognition of his mastery of Italy from the Byzantine Empire (see p. 104). Theodoric continued the synthesis of barbarian military power and Roman administration, but he governed a society which could no longer truly be considered "Roman."

Between 535 and 554, the Byzantine Emperor Justinian recaptured much of barbarian Italy, expelling the Ostrogoths and establishing a new Western imperial capital at Ravenna in northern Italy. Rome itself lay in ruins, and any semblance of the city's old imperial government had vanished. In the seventh century when the Byzantines began to retreat from Italy, Roman unity simply collapsed. Italy saw itself divided into principalities ruled by barbarian kings.

Unity: A Desperate Need

Faced with the frightening collapse of Western society, the Western Church had to focus its energies around a single unifying force in order to survive as a working institution. That force was the papacy. While valid judgments can be made about the overextension and corruption of papal power in the late Middle Ages (a topic treated in another volume in this series), condemnations of papal "usurpation of power" are out of place at this early date.

The first pope truly to unify the Western bishops under his headship so as to form a centrally organized Western Church was Pope Leo the Great (440-461). We have already considered Leo's theological contribution (see Chapter Seven). Along with his participation in the Christological debate, Leo took great interest in developing the theory of papal primacy. Leo saw Christ as the Church's true and eternal bishop, and taught that Christ conferred his episcopal authority first and foremost on Peter (the "Rock").

Just as Christ is the eternal shepherd, Leo taught, so too, Peter is his eternal vicar on earth, who exercises his authority throughout history in the Bishops of Rome. Leo saw the popes as "heirs" of Peter, entitled to all of Peter's authority and subject to all of his responsibility. Since Jesus in Matthew 16:18 conferred upon Peter first rank among the Apostles, Leo said, the Bishop of Rome, as Peter's heir, stands first among the other bishops. Owing to the collapse of order in the West, few Western bishops were in a position to challenge Leo's theory, which came to be universally accepted in the West.

Only Bishop Hilary of Arles (403-449) challenged Leo's claim to primacy. In 444 Hilary deposed a bishop in his province. The latter appealed directly to Leo, who saw in the dispute an opportunity to put his theory of papal primacy into practice. Leo stripped Hilary of his title as metropolitan (chief bishop) of his province, and convinced Emperor Valentinian III to decree that the Roman bishop exercised supreme control of the Church in France.

The importance of this affair is seen in Hilary's submission to Leo's authority. In the East such a controversy would no doubt have led to immediate mutual excommunications and a protracted schism. In the West, however, where everyone recognized that unity was a desperate need, bishops who disagreed with each other did not square off into anathematizing fisticuffs. Out of necessity, the Western bishops assented to the pope's authority. They did not necessarily consider the pope's word to be final because it was right, but right because it was final—*for unity's sake*.

The 'Two-Power' Theory

Another fifth-century pope, Gelasius I (492-496), elaborated upon Leo's theories and continued to expand papal power. Gelasius developed the "two-power theory" of earthly authority which later came to dominate medieval political thinking.

According to Gelasius all earthly power has been given to pope and emperor. Since to the pope is given the direction of "divine things," he is superior to the emperor, who is supreme only in civil matters. (Notice how radically this theory differs from that of Eusebius of Caesarea in the East, discussed on p. 57.) As might be expected, Gelasius' theory drew harsh criticism from Constantinople. But in Rome the Ostrogoth King Theodoric the Great accorded the pope great respect, guaranteeing the Roman see his personal protection.

The significance of Gelasius' theory of papal primacy was twofold: (1) Gelasius gained lasting approval in the West for the notion that the pope was the arbiter of *doctrinal* disputes; and (2) through the papacy Gelasius established the Church as a power equal to and independent of the state. Under Gelasius, the Western Church's long struggle for autonomy from the Empire reached a victorious conclusion.

East and West were now set on different courses. Henceforth in the West it would be the State, *not* the Church, which would strive for independence in the Church-State relationship. In the East, where Gelasius' "two-power theory" was rejected, the emperor continued his dominance of the Church.

Pope Gregory the Great

Under Pope Gregory the Great (590-604) the papacy reached the pinnacle of prestige and influence. Gregory, the great-grandson of Pope Felix II, came from one of Rome's oldest families. Like Ambrose in the fourth century, Gregory at first pursued a career in government, and eventually rose to occupy the equivalent of Rome's mayoralty. He then rejected political life and founded a monastery where he lived until 579. (We take up monasticism on p. 145.) Gregory adhered to Gelasius' "two-power theory," but tried to smoothe over relations with the East by speaking and writing favorably of the Byzantine emperor.

Gregory also displayed a conciliatory and brotherly attitude toward other bishops, declining the title which other fifth-century popes had taken—"Universal Bishop"—in favor of the less pretentious, "Servant of the Servants of God." Nonetheless, Gregory showed himself to be a rigorous advocate of papal primacy, as when he wrote:

> To all who know the gospel it is obvious that by the voice of the Lord the care of the entire Church was committed to the holy apostle and prince of all the apostles, Peter....Am I defending my own cause in this matter? Am I vindicating some special injury of my own? Is it not rather the cause of Almighty God, the cause of the universal Church?...And we certainly know that many priests of the Church of Constantinople have fallen into the whirlpool of heresy and have become heretics. Certainly in honor of Peter, the prince of the apostles, the title "universal" was offered to the Roman pontiff by the venerable Council of Chalcedon.[13]

Although Gregory saw himself as heir of Peter, he was first and foremost a priest and a pastor in his personal life. Through him the Church took over from the State the task of providing for the needs of the poor and the outcast. Gregory personally attended to the establishment of hospitals and orphanages, and regarded it as an integral part of his duties as pope to nurse the sick, visit prisoners, care for orphans and offer counsel to widows and the elderly. He admonished his fellow priests for their laxity, and began to upgrade their spiritual and intellectual preparation. It was Gregory who established the principle that every Mass should contain a sermon on Scripture.

A true monk at heart, Gregory likewise sought to reform

monasticism and to strengthen monastic spirituality by writing about contemplative prayer and asceticism. Realizing that the Church could not survive if it clung to the past, Gregory encouraged monks and priests to venture into the barbarian hinterlands to make new converts. Gregory was thus the first pope to sponsor extensive missionary campaigns. It was Gregory, for example, who sent Augustine of Canterbury (not the same Augustine we take up in the next chapter) to organize the Church in England.

This brief survey of the events of Western Church history after Constantine roughly brings us to the same point in time where we terminated our discussion of the Eastern Church in the last chapter. Let's stop for a moment and compare the two branches of the Church as they are poised to enter the Middle Ages. While we have not yet discussed Augustine (who lived before Gregory), a comparison at this point will help to introduce the significance of Augustine's thought to the future development of Western Christianity.

TOWARD THE MIDDLE AGES:
DIFFERENT PATHS OF EAST AND WEST

The Eastern and Western Churches pursued different paths in the area of Church-State relations as well as different approaches to theology and doctrine. We can illustrate this difference by comparing the writings of Pope Gregory the Great and the philosopher Boethius (c. 450-524) in the West, to the writings of Emperor Justinian and the theologian known as Pseudo-Dionysius (c. 500) in the East.

Rational vs. Mystical

In the realm of Christian thought Pope Gregory and Emperor Justinian made significant contributions. Justinian, true to the Eastern tradition, wrote speculative treatises on Christology, while Gregory confined himself to more practical matters. Gregory wrote on everyday topics such as fasting, penance and satisfaction for sin—which he believed could be achieved even after death in *purgatory*. Gregory's writings helped make Augustine's thought comprehensible to the average Christian.

Gregory elevated Augustine's speculations on purgatory to the level of doctrine, declaring purgatory to be something in which orthodox Christians must believe. In his writings on purgatory, Gregory laid the foundation for the medieval concept of accumulated spiritual *merit*. The prayers of the faithful, and participation in the sacrifice of the Mass, served to "store," as it were, Christ's salvific energy in the Church, where it could be released at a later time to absolve both living and dead from their sins.

Boethius laid the foundation for the medieval Western Church's theological method by focusing on what he called "theological reason," in which he sought to ground the truths of theology in philosophy. Accordingly, he defined such traditional theological concepts as "person," "substance" and "being" in ways that removed them from their purely theological context, pointing the way for the medieval Schoolmen to develop intricate syntheses of philosophy and theology.

In contrast to the *rational* emphasis given to Western theology by Boethius, Pseudo-Dionysius developed a *mystical* theology which has characterized Orthodox spirituality to this day. Pseudo-Dionysius, an anonymous sixth-century writer who wrote under the name of Dionysius the Areopagite (see Acts 17:34), convinced most people of his day that his writings actually dated to St. Paul's time.

Pseudo-Dionysius taught that even in this life Christians can achieve mystical union with God. Through Pope Gregory, this thought passed into the Western tradition where later it was reinterpreted in the Middle Ages by Bernard of Clairvaux and Thomas Aquinas.

At the turn of the seventh century, we find the early Church divided by Latin and Greek culture, language and thought. The Western Church entered the Middle Ages led by the papacy as successor to Roman imperial authority, and characterized by a practical philosophical outlook. It thus became expansive, rationalistic and universalist. The Eastern Church, on the other hand, turned introspective and conservative. Fanning the dying embers of Empire, it extended its frontiers not to the outer geographical limits of the known world, as did the West, but to the *inner* contemplative reaches of the indwelling Spirit.

'Animus' vs. 'Anima'

In psychological terms, we could say that the West developed the Church's *animus* (the male traits of dominance, intellect and analysis), while the East developed the Church's *anima* (the female traits of receptivity, intuition and synthesis). Just as no human being is whole without both *animus* and *anima*, so too the Church entered the Middle Ages in danger of developing a fractured personality. The intellectual and spiritual history of the medieval Church is largely a story of the Church's quest for its lost wholeness (the story of the next volume).

For now, we turn to Augustine of Hippo, who almost single-handedly constructs the conceptual framework within which the story of the medieval Church will unfold. His life is stamped on virtually every page of later Church thought and belief.

TIMELINE: 312 A.D. —600 A.D.

312: Christianity becomes "favored" religion of the Empire

321: Arius is excommunicated
325: Council and Creed of Nicaea   324: Constantine rules a reunited empire
328: Athanasius becomes Bishop of Alexandria

335: Synod of Tyre results in exile of Athanasius
337: Empire divided among Constantine's sons; Donatists have become major party in North Africa

350: Arian Constantine II becomes sole emperor
353: Synod of Arles condemns Athanasius

360: Synod of Constantinople ratifies the Arian Homoian Creed, nullifying Nicene Creed

373: Basil the Great refutes the Pneumatomachians   374: Ambrose chosen as Bishop of Milan

378: Battle of Adrianople
381: Council and Creed of Constantinople   380: Christianity as defended by Athanasius
383: First monastery in the West   and Cappadocians decreed "official"
387: Augustine embraces Christianity   religion by Theodosius

400

405: Edict of Union which suppresses Donatists in North Africa; Pelagius begins preaching in Rome
410: Alaric the Visigoth sacks Rome   411: Synod of Carthage outlaws Donatism

418: Synod of Carthage condemns Pelagius

430: Bishops Cyril and Nestorius feud over *Theotokos*   431: Council of Ephesus
433: Formula of Union

444: Hilary of Arles's submission to Pope Leo illustrates consolidation of papal authority in the West
448: Synod of Constantinople condemns Eutyches's one-nature Christology

Marcian (450–457)

451: Council and Creed of Chalcedon

457: Marcian's death triggers resurgence of Monophysitism

Prosper of Aquitaine (c.463)
Theodoret of Cyrrhus (c.466)

Gelasius I (492-496)

489: Ostrogoth Theodoric conquers Italy
By this point, term *Roman Empire* no longer pertains
Barbarians rule in the West; Byzantine Empire in the East

Boniface II (530-532)

525: Benedict founds Monte Cassino, writes *Rule*
529: Synod of Orange defends the core of Augustine's teaching

Boethius (c.524)

553: Second Council of Constantinople fails to reconcile Chalcedonians and Monophysites

Justinian (527-565)

589: Third Council of Toledo (589)

Private penance in West spreads from Ireland to continent

Gregory the Great (590-604)

600: Apostles' Creed in use in the West

Gregory of Tours (c.594)

500

Single dates in parentheses indicate an individual's date of death; dates spanning a number of years refer to time in office.

CHAPTER NINE

'This Man Taught Us Everything'

Augustine's Contribution to His Age and Beyond

Augustine was born in 354 at Thagaste in Numidia, a region of North Africa known for its rigorism in matters of Church discipline. His mother Monica was a devout Catholic. His father Patrick was a lifelong pagan until he accepted Christian baptism on his deathbed.

Augustine rejected his mother's religion because to him it seemed intellectually vacuous. He could not accept a religion which professed no more profound a solution to the problem of good and evil than to proclaim that God sent his Son into the world to die for humanity's sin. As someone educated in the great works of antiquity, Augustine sought for a nobler answer to his questions about God, the world and the relationship between the two.

Augustine became attracted to an Eastern religion known as Manicheism (a quasi-Gnostic sect from Persia), which taught the existence of two separate absolute powers—one good, the other evil. Manicheans followed the path of renunciation, and required strenuous fasting and sexual continence of members. The latter requirement precluded Augustine's wholehearted entrance into the cult because he was very much a man of his times in the area of sexual promiscuity.

What ultimately drove Augustine out of the movement, however, was Manicheism's logical inconsistency as well as Augustine's disappointment with the mediocre personal qualities of its members. In his *Confessions* Augustine described his meeting with a famous Manichean elder, who left him unimpressed:

> I found him to be a man of pleasant speech, who spoke of the very same things as they [the other Manicheans] themselves did, although more fluently and in better language.

> ...My ears were already satiated with similar things; neither did they appear to me more conclusive because better expressed; nor true because oratorical; nor the spirit necessarily wise because the face was comely and the language eloquent.[1]

By 383 Augustine's life was something of a shambles. He had found no belief system capable of satisfying his driving search for meaning in life. Further, his sexual promiscuity had left him feeling shallow and unfulfilled. He felt trapped by his compulsive lusts, unable to free himself from their jealous demands. In a spirit of frustration, he moved with his son (borne him by his North African mistress) to Milan, where he accepted a teaching position in rhetoric.

In Milan Augustine heard good reports from his pagan friends concerning the rhetorical abilities of Ambrose, Milan's Christian bishop. Always eager to learn new techniques of argumentation, Augustine went to hear Ambrose preach at the cathedral. He received much more than he had expected. Although moved by Ambrose's oratorical eloquence, Augustine was even more impressed by the substance of Ambrose's words. He found in them a presentation of the gospel that captured both his heart and his mind.

Yet Augustine came away from his encounters with Ambrose feeling even more dejected. His intellect had been won by the gospel, but his body was still the prisoner of sexual incontinence. Augustine must have come to a deep existential understanding of the Apostle Paul's words, "I am weak flesh sold into the slavery of sin. I cannot even understand my own actions. I do not do what I want to do but what I hate" (Romans 7:14b-15). As Augustine remembered it later, he did not even have the power to *pray* for release from his bondage. "Grant me chastity and continence, Lord," his soul urged, "but not yet."

Augustine finally admitted defeat and humbly turned the battle over to a stronger Warrior. Sequestering himself in a Milanese garden, Augustine poured out his heart to the Christ he had come to know through Ambrose's preaching. Weeping bitterly, he thought he heard a child's voice singing, "Take and read, take and read..." over and over again. Picking up the Scriptures, Augustine's eyes fell immediately on Paul's words, "...not in carousing and drunkenness, not in sexual excess and lust, not in quarreling and jealousy. Rather, put on the Lord Jesus Christ and make no provision for the desires of the flesh" (Romans 13:13b-14).

Augustine's battle had ended. At that very moment he felt the power of the gospel—"The power of God leading everyone who believes in it to salvation" (Romans 1:16)—penetrate his entire being. "No further would I read," he wrote in his *Confessions*, "nor did I need; for instantly, as the sentence ended, by a light, as it were, of security into my heart, all the gloom of doubt vanished away."[2]

Like the Apostle Paul before him, Augustine needed time to deliberate on the meaning of his sudden conversion experience. He withdrew with friends to a quiet retreat outside of Milan known as Cassiciacum. There he wrote dialogues on the great spiritual questions which had dominated his life.

CHRISTIAN PLATONIST: A CREATIVE SYNTHESIS

Augustine, even though a Westerner, approached his inquiries into the mysteries of the gospel from a Platonic perspective. Earlier Western writers, such as Tertullian, had relied more on the Stoic, pragmatic approach. But by Augustine's time Western thinkers had become well versed in the Platonic debates taking place in the East. Easterners (like Athanasius) and Westerners exiled to the East (like Hilary of Poitiers) had transmitted the Eastern "idiom" to the West.

Thus Augustine used Platonism to express his newfound belief in the superiority of the Christian gospel. Throughout his life he was to remain a Christian Platonist. It was his synthesis of philosophy and the gospel that served as a vehicle for the transmission of Augustine's work to the Middle Ages.

Augustine's Approach to the Trinity

Augustine's most creative adaptation of Platonism is found in his work on the Trinity. Platonism saw God's presence exemplified in all creation. Likewise Augustine saw the imprint of the Trinity present throughout creation and in humanity itself. Augustine finds this *Trinitarian vestige* best illustrated in the human faculties of *memory, understanding* and *will*.

Just as these three faculties express themselves in one human mind, so too the three divine persons express but a single Godhead. One *remembers* that one understands and wills; one *understands* that one wills and remembers; and one *wills* to remember and understand. In all three operations, however, only a *single mind* functions. Moreover, as one remembers one does not at the same time cease to understand and will, and so on.

Although we *speak* of memory, understanding and will as separate, we do this because we perceive the three operations to be separate in their effect. Our language unfortunately belies the essential unity of mind which underlies the three.

Likewise our language compels us to speak of "Father, Son and Holy Spirit" when referring to God. But God's essential unity is not actually compartmentalized. It is because our minds are bounded by time and space that we must speak of the One God as if he were "triple," when in reality the triune God is actually one.

For Augustine the *entire* Trinity is involved in the action of *each* of its persons. As Augustine put it, "The operation of the Trinity is inseparable in each of those things which are said to pertain to the manifesting of *either* the Father, *or* the Son, *or* the Holy Spirit."[3] When we say "the Father did this" or "the Son did that," we are simply *appropriating* God's action to one person of the Trinity. This is necessary to our own understanding of God's action, but it does not accurately express God's true nature. In actuality, "The Trinity *together* wrought both the voice of the Father, and the flesh of the Son, and the dove of the Holy Spirit, while each of these things is *referred severally* to each person" (emphasis added).[4]

The relationship between the three human faculties of memory, understanding and will likewise helps us to understand the *relationship* between the three divine persons. Memory can be called memory only in reference to something else, and the same is true of understanding and will.

In the same way the Father is only Father insofar as he begets the Son, and the Son is only Son insofar as he has a Father. The relationship between the three persons is eternal. The Father has ceaselessly begotten the Son, while there was never a time when the Son was not Son. The Holy Spirit is the love bond uniting the Father and Son in their eternal relationship.

As the Father begets the Son, and as the Son participates in divine communion with the Father, their act of intercommunion itself is divine and eternal and "a substance"[5] which we identify as the Holy Spirit. The Holy Spirit, then, proceeds not from the Father only, as the Creed of Constantinople put it, but from the Father *and* the Son. It was thus Augustine who introduced the *filioque* ("and the Son") doctrine into Christian thought. In the Middle Ages the Eastern Church was to condemn this extension of Trinitarian theology beyond the actual words of the Constantinopolitan Creed.

For Augustine, therefore, the Trinity is principally *relationship*. Whereas the Cappadocians, in order to combat the heresies of their time, had concerned themselves more with the natures of the *individual persons* (see page 75), Augustine stresses the divine *unity*. He is reluctant even to theorize about a single person in the Trinity apart from that

126

person's relationship to the other two. "It is hard to see," he wrote, "how we can say either the Father alone, or the Son alone, since both the Father is with the Son, and the Son with the Father, always and inseparably."[6]

Augustine and the Great Theological Debates

Augustine was baptized a Christian six years after the Council of Constantinople (381) and died the year before the Council of Ephesus (431). What a pity that the chronology of Augustine's life prevented him from taking part in these two councils! The history of Christian thought sorely lacks a recorded confrontation between the great Western master and the spokesmen for the various Eastern theories on the incarnation and the Trinity.

Where would Augustine have placed himself in the Eastern debate? It may seem to us that Augustine's Trinitarian theology skirts dangerously close to Sabellianism; that is, he seems almost to allow the Son's identity to get "absorbed" into the one, transcendent God. Yet, Augustine is *not* saying that the existence of three distinct persons is an illusion by which God *seems* to be triune. To return to Augustine's favorite model: memory, intellect and will are not illusory; each is a true expression of the one mind. In the same way the three divine persons possess their own identities.

Owing to our incapacity to *conceptualize* triune diversity-in-unity, we often err either by going to the extreme of Sabellianism (in which all diversity is absorbed), or to the extreme of Subordinationism (in which the unity is shattered). Augustine avoided both extremes. He expounded upon Christianity's greatest mystery as precisely as could be done in human language.

BISHOP OF HIPPO: THREE CHALLENGES

After his baptism by Ambrose in 387 and his retreat at Cassiciacum, Augustine returned in 388 to Thagaste in North Africa. There he established an ascetic community and began to live a contemplative life. In 391 he traveled to Hippo in order to persuade a friend to join the community in Thagaste. Augustine's reputation had preceded him, however, and the Catholics in Hippo insisted that he become a priest in their local church.

Bishop Valerius of Hippo obliged his flock, and ordained Augustine a priest practically on the spot. Four years later Valerius installed Augustine as his coadjutor bishop, and when the old man died in 396, Augustine succeeded him as chief shepherd of the Catholic community in Hippo. Until his death in 430 Augustine served as bishop, giving up all dreams of returning to the contemplative life which he had left behind in Thagaste.

It was as bishop that Augustine's great talents were particularly made manifest. His abstract intelligence, blended with his diplomatic and rhetorical skills, made him both a great administrator and the champion of Catholic orthodoxy.

Augustine's gifts were sorely needed. Three great crises would challenge his episcopacy: Donatism, Pelagianism and the breakdown of the Roman state. In mastering each challenge Augustine established doctrinal principles whose effect far transcended the boundaries of his own day and age. Let us look briefly at the three major concerns of Augustine's tenure as bishop (395-430).

The Donatist Controversy

We left the Donatist controversy early in the fourth century (see p. 55). Constantine had tried to resolve the dispute between Donatists and Catholics, but by 320 he had practically given up any hope of reconciling the two groups. In 321 he wrote to the Catholic bishops of North Africa asking them to tolerate the schismatic Donatist Church. From that time on the two Churches increasingly went their separate ways. By Constantine's death it was no longer a question of Catholics tolerating Donatists, but the other way around. The Donatist Church by 337 had become the *majority* Christian party in North Africa.

The Donatists grew both more powerful and more aggressive. By 340 they had attracted into their ranks bellicose Berber tribesmen whose culture had no conception of religious tolerance. These *Circumcellions* (they practiced a ritual of processing *circum cellas*—"around the shrines"—of famous North African martyrs) attacked and murdered Catholics, burned down their churches and, if cornered by Roman police, fanatically committed suicide.

In 347 a Donatist bishop exercised poor judgment for his cause by organizing the Circumcellions into a kind of paramilitary resistance force for attacking Roman troops. The rebels were summarily annihilated (and speedily taken into the ranks of Donatist martyrs). Each such incident made the Donatists more fanatically intransigent. They expressed their belief in the slogan, "Great is the Church of the Numidians: We are the Christians, only we."[7]

The key to the Donatist position was the belief that the sacraments were only valid *ex opere operantis*—that is, only on the basis of the sacramental minister's personal holiness. Since the time of Bishop Stephen the Catholics had favored the contrary position of sacramental validity: *ex opere operato*—that is, based on the action itself. In the

Catholic view, the validity of a sacrament depended not on the minister, but on Christ himself who worked through the minister.

According to the Donatists, Catholic clergy who apostatized during the great persecution had rendered themselves incapable of administering valid sacraments. Further, any bishop in communion with them had likewise become tinged with impurity. Thus, for the Donatists the Catholic Church's entire sacramental ministry was illegitimate. By the time Augustine became bishop the Donatists had come to see Catholicism as the apotheosis of evil.

To combat the Donatist hostility, Augustine decided to ignore the Donatists' personality attacks in favor of a reasoned argument based on theological principle. The basis of his counteroffensive was to distinguish between objective and subjective sacramental validity.

For example, Augustine said: "All men possess Baptism who have received it in any place, from any sort of man, just so long as it was consecrated with the words of the gospel and was received by them without deceit and with some degree of faith."[8] Augustine contrasted such objective criteria to the subjective criterion of "the conscience of the giver," which he rejected as unnecessary for sacramental validity.

Augustine went on to say, however, that although a sacrament is valid, it may not be *effective*. The effectiveness of a sacrament—its function as a channel of grace—depends upon one's union with the Catholic Church. The Donatists made one's union with the Church contingent upon one's holiness; but Augustine saw the holiness of individual Christians as dependent upon their union with the Church.

Augustine in no way saw minimalistic, superficial Church membership and reception of the sacraments as a guarantee of holiness and union with the Church. On the contrary, Augustine taught that those who participated in the sacraments were not necessarily united to the Church. Thus, whereas he posited an objective theory of the sacraments, Augustine rejected the notion that one could make an objective evaluation of one's state of communion with the Church.

In a famous maxim Augustine said, "There are many whom the Catholic Church has that God does not have, and many that God has whom the Catholic Church does not have." It was this viewpoint which made possible a reconciliation between Catholics and Donatists.

By his objective sacramental theology Augustine admitted the validity (though not the effectiveness) of Donatist sacraments. On the other hand, he avoided equating membership in the institutional Catholic Church with salvation. This opened the door for Donatists to resubmit to Catholic discipline without having to admit that in the Donatist Church they had lived outside of God's favor. In a spirit of peace and goodwill

Augustine professed that the only requirement for Donatist reentry into the Catholic Church was the imposition of hands by the Catholic priest or bishop on the returning brother or sister.

Augustine and the other North African Catholic bishops invited the Donatist bishops to meet with them in a series of synods. The Catholic offer was spurned repeatedly and rudely, as when the Donatist bishop Primian explained his refusal to attend a synod in 403 with the statement, "It is contrary to the dignity of the sons of martyrs to meet with the descendants of *traditores*."[9] (Primian was referring here to the origins of the quarrel nearly a century before, in which a Catholic bishop had been consecrated by a *traditore*—that is, a bishop who had cooperated with the Roman police during Diocletian's persecution. See p. 55.)

The Donatists refused to "forgive and forget." Far from attempting to reconcile with the Catholics, the Donatists even stepped up their acts of violence. Eventually, and solely for protection, the Catholic bishops asked for imperial military support of the Catholic party.

When Emperor Honorius (395-423) reviewed the situation, however, he decided on a policy of full-scale repression of the Donatist Church. In 405 he issued an Edict of Union in which he branded the Donatists as heretics and ordered them to transfer their churches to the Catholics. It had now become clear to everyone that a peaceful solution was impossible. Augustine reluctantly supported the use of force, justifying his position with reference to Luke 14:23: "Go out into the highways and along the hedgerows and *force* them to come in" (emphasis added).

In 411 the emperor's legate invited Donatist and Catholic bishops to a final synod on the controversy at Carthage. This time the Donatists attended. The Catholic bishops took every conceivable step to assure the Donatists of an impartial decision and to establish a conciliatory atmosphere. Yet, when the Donatists arrived they refused to sit in the presence of "the ungodly," and focused their entire argument on the minute insults and offenses which had occurred during the previous century.

Finally, after two days of rancorous accusations, the Donatists made their theological argument. Augustine was at last given his opportunity to debate the substantive issues, and he quickly established himself as the dominant authority on the entire subject. At the close of the debate the emperor's legate decided for the Catholics and against the Donatists. Donatism was outlawed, though it did not disappear. Not until the onslaught of the Moslems in the seventh century did Donatism vanish from the sands of Africa.

The Pelagian Controversy

In the Donatist controversy Augustine confronted a distorted teaching on the *means* of grace; in the Pelagian controversy he opposed a teaching which questioned the very *necessity* of grace. If you have never read Augustine before, I predict that you are about to be shocked by his response to the Pelagian challenge. Many have said that Pelagianism is still the predominate heresy of our time—and Augustine's thoughts will sound terribly threatening to our 20th-century belief in individual will power and personal self-improvement.

Pelagius—from whom the heresy of Pelagianism took its name—was a native of Britain and is thought to have been a monk. About the year 405 he traveled to Rome and established himself as a preacher of some repute, associating himself with a lawyer named Celestius who tried to write systematic statements of Pelagius's thought.

Pelagius once heard a bishop preach a sermon quoting Augustine's prayer, "Lord, grant what you command, and command what you will." This statement made Pelagius very uneasy, and upon looking more deeply into Augustine's writings, he thought he found there a system in which the necessity for human moral effort was eliminated. Since Pelagius believed human beings could be good solely through their own efforts, he sensed in Augustine's writings a distorted emphasis on God's grace. He concluded that Augustine taught a "grace-only" morality.

The essential difference between Augustine and Pelagius was their contrasting understanding of grace. For Augustine, grace is God's own power enabling humanity to live uprightly. Grace is entirely God's prerogative and is manifested in human life only when God on his own initiative so chooses. For Augustine, humanity by itself—without God's grace—lacks the power *not* to sin. Thus, before a Christian can produce any good work, he or she must first be moved by God's grace. As a result, the first impulse toward salvation comes from God, and never from humanity.

Pelagius denied neither the existence nor effectiveness of grace. He believed, however, that all the grace humanity ever needed was released into the world at creation. This "grace of creation" was available to anyone who wanted it simply by the assertion of one's free will in the direction of good. Thus, for Pelagius, one's freely chosen decision for good is the first step toward salvation, and everyone has the capacity to take this step. (In a sense this step is also based on "grace" since the very ability to make such a decision stems from God's grace of creation. When Pelagius got backed into a corner he would therefore agree with Augustine that the ability to do good is a gift of God. He parted company with Augustine, however, by teaching that the *will* to do good, and the good *act* itself come from the individual's free decision.)

The controversy between Augustine and Pelagius inevitably led to the question, "Who can be saved?"

Augustine believed that only a minority of people would actually receive God's grace and be saved. The majority are eternally damned from the moment of conception. This was Augustine's famous and troublesome concept of predestination.

In response to those who criticized his harsh view of God's justice, Augustine pointed out that God did not damn people. In reality, he said, people are already damned because of original sin. God in his mercy intervenes to save a portion of this "mass of damnation." We should be grateful for what God *does*, Augustine urged, and not bemoan what he does *not* do in refusing the grace of salvation to some.

"Is there such a thing as free will?" Augustine's critics asked. "Or are the damned irresistibly condemned to a life of sin while the elect are irresistibly motivated to holiness?"

Augustine believed in free will, but saw it as an integrated aspect of fallen human nature. Until God's grace illumines the soul, free will can only choose evil. After God's illumination free will has the power to do good and, since good can only seek good, the graced soul will inevitably choose the path of righteousness.

Pelagius rejected Augustine's understanding of both predestination and free will. For Pelagius, sin resulted not from a hereditary disability traced back to Adam, but simply from the imitation of bad actions which people see going on all around them. Both Pelagius and Augustine believed in infant baptism. But Pelagius saw it simply as the Church's means of bestowing God's "blessing" on the newborn, whereas Augustine saw it as necessary for salvation. Pelagius denied that an unbaptized person who performed good works was excluded from heaven.

Pelagius's view of Baptism eventually led to his condemnation. At the Synod of Carthage in 418 the Catholic bishops condemned "anyone who denies that newborn infants are to be baptized or who says that they are baptized for the remission of sins but do not bear anything of original sin from Adam which is expiated by the washing of regeneration."[10]

If one were to read representative selections of Augustine's and Pelagius's works to a randomly selected audience of educated Americans, more hands would be raised in support of Pelagius than Augustine. Augustine's teaching flies in the face of the secular humanism which is the basis of 20th-century American life. We believe that humanity, and not God, is the motivating force behind the universe.

Likewise we believe that unimpeded human effort can accomplish all things. Sin—if it exists—is not an inherent human condition but an imprudent action resulting from poor blood chemistry, not enough coffee in the morning, "stress," or poor toilet training in our early years. Augustine's teaching seems cruel and barbaric. In place of his gospel of grace we prefer the gospel of self-development.

Augustine's teaching on grace, predestination and free will was rebutted by Catholic thinkers even in his own day. Augustine himself gave his teaching a second glance and, toward the end of his life, seemed to modify his views, as when he wrote, "The *capacity* to have faith, as the *capacity* to have love, belongs to man's nature; but to *have* faith, even as to *have* love, belongs to the grace of believers."[11] Later in this chapter we will look at the debate which took place over Augustine's teachings and see how the Church softened the harsh edges of Augustine's teaching on grace.

Yet the Church steadfastly held to its doctrine of original sin. Nor was Augustine the first to defend this doctrine. From the early second century onward Christian thinkers preached the Apostles' belief that "through one man sin entered the world" (Romans 5:12).

The Church's teaching on original sin is perhaps the most abhorrent Christian doctrine in a Pelagian "me-first" culture such as ours. It flies in the face of our unlimited self-reliance, and forces us to acknowledge that we cannot save ourselves. Perhaps a rereading of Augustine's teachings will lead the 20th century out of its present predicament. Like Augustine we may have to face the harsh reality that we cannot extricate ourselves from the consequences of our own choices, and like him cry out, "Our hearts are restless, O Lord, until they rest in you."

The 'City of God' vs. the 'Earthly City'

The final crisis faced by Bishop Augustine was caused by the barbarian conquest of the Roman Empire. When the Visigoths sacked Rome in 410, pagans blamed the disaster on the Empire's rejection of the ancient religion and its acceptance of Christianity. Since Christians themselves were good Roman citizens, they too wondered how the very institution which God had chosen to spread his kingdom on earth could have been humiliated by the barbarians. In *The City of God*, Augustine tried to provide an answer.

In *The City of God*, Augustine developed a model to illustrate his political and social theory. His model was that of two cities existing in such a way that they are closely united externally, but vastly different in their respective purposes and values. The two cities are "the city of God" and "the earthly city." The first is made up of those predestined to salvation; the second, of those predestined to damnation. The values, life-styles and goals of the two cities are radically opposed to each other. The "city of God" is founded on love, selflessness and service to others; citizens of the earthly city seek only their own gratification.

Like the wheat and the tares, the two cities exist inseparably until the final judgment. Then their deeds will be made manifest and their conduct rewarded. The purpose of the State is to provide sufficient order for the city of God to pursue its interests.

When the State oversteps its authority by fostering the interests of the earthly city to the detriment of the city of God, Christians must nonetheless support the political authorities—up to the point where the authorities command disobedience to God's law. When that point is reached, Christians may not rebel, but must accept the injustice and persecution which will naturally follow from their refusal to sin. Oppression by the State should be seen as a sign of God's punishment for sin. Even in the face of persecution Christians should continue praying for the authorities' conversion.

Augustine said that one cannot judge objectively whether worldly strife and chaos—such as the barbarian invasions—are good or bad. God may very well have used the invasions as a means to punish the Empire for its sins and to provide an opportunity for the Church to make new converts. Thus Christians are not to despair. They are to accept whatever punishment God sends them and pray for the restoration of peace and order. In this way the city of God will once again be able to pursue its task of bringing people to salvation.

Augustine followed his own advice. With the Vandals battering down the walls of Hippo, he stayed on to shepherd his besieged flock, allowing only enough of his priests to escape to serve outlying regions. Augustine died on August 28, 430, shortly before the invaders entered Hippo.

THE AUGUSTINIAN SYNTHESIS:
TOWARD THE MIDDLE AGES

Not everyone accepted Augustine's teaching on grace, predestination and free will. Most of those who disagreed with him were loyal Catholics. Further, most of those who questioned his orthodoxy in these areas unhesitatingly accepted his teachings in other areas, such as his Trinitarian teaching.

Semi-Pelagianism

The principal criticism of Augustine's views on grace was undertaken by monks living in southern France who were associated with Abbot John Cassian (c. 360-435). Cassian had been born in the East and in his youth joined a monastery in Bethlehem. After a brief stint as a deacon in Constantinople he eventually migrated to France, founding two monasteries near Marseilles. He wrote a work called *The Institutes* in which he discussed monastic discipline. Benedict of Nursia (whom we discuss in the next chapter), the father of Western monasticism, was to incorporate much of Cassian's thought (and thus Eastern monastic theory) into his famous *Rule*.

Cassian was the founder of a school of thought which has come to be known as Semi-Pelagianism. Cassian tried to steer a middle course between Augustine's "grace-only" view and Pelagius's "nature-only" perspective. Although Cassian and the other Semi-Pelagians agreed with Augustine that grace was necessary for salvation, they argued that Augustine emphasized grace to the exclusion of free will.

For Cassian salvation was not an either-or issue; he believed that both the impulse of grace and the assent of the will were necessary. For Cassian questions about the respective priorities in time of grace and will were pointless. As he explained the matter, "As soon as God sees in us the beginning of a good will, he illumines, stimulates, and urges it towards salvation, giving growth to that which he himself planted, or to that which he has seen spring out of our own effort."[12]

Cassian believed that human effort has a role to play in salvation; therefore he rejected Augustine's teaching on predestination and free will. Basing his argument on such Scripture verses as 1 Timothy 2:4—"[God] wants *all* men to be saved"—Cassian asked, "How can we imagine without grievous blasphemy that God does not desire all men in general, but only some rather than all to be saved?"[13] To think as Augustine did, Cassian wrote, meant that God took people's wills captive, restricting the free exercise of his greatest gift, the capacity to make a knowing choice for or against God.

Probably the most articulate spokesman for the Semi-Pelagian point of view was Faustus of Riez (c. 408-490), a British monk who lived at a monastery on the Isle of Lerins in the Mediterranean, near today's Cannes. In his treatise *On Grace*, Faustus became an even more outspoken defender of free will and human effort than Cassian had been. Faustus read Scripture as a chronicle of the partnership between God's grace and human effort. He saw Augustine's teaching as a "fatalistic theory."

Faustus criticized Augustine's doctrine of predestination by arguing that Augustine misunderstood the difference between God's foreknowledge and God's will. Although God may *know* in advance that a portion of humanity will be damned, Faustus said, this does not mean that God *wills* damnation. To think otherwise, Faustus argued, would make the Church, the sacraments and the preaching of the gospel pointless. Why bother to evangelize or administer God's grace to people who are already either irrevocably saved or damned?

Augustine's Defenders

Augustine's defenders rushed to his assistance. The greatest Augustinian apologist was Prosper of Aquitaine (c. 390-463). Like the Semi-Pelagians, he lived a monastic life near Marseilles. Prosper introduced Augustine himself to the Semi-Pelagian criticism, thereby affording Augustine the opportunity to write two treatises in his own defense before he died.

After Augustine's death Prosper carried his defense of Augustine to Rome, where Pope Celestine I offered his encouragement. Prosper wrote harsh criticism of Semi-Pelagianism, but eventually began to moderate his position. In the evolution of Prosper's thought we find the origins of an Augustinian synthesis, which reconciled the great master's own doctrine to the Semi-Pelagian reaction.

He took the traditional Augustinian stance that the mystery of salvation resided in the mind of God. Gradually, however, he began to modify the definition of predestination. Whereas Augustine had taught that only a minority were saved, Prosper got away from the vexing controversy over numbers altogether. He admitted that "there is *no one* to whom either the preaching of the gospel or the commandments of the law or the voice of nature does not transmit God's call."[14] This moved the Augustinian position much closer to that of the Semi-Pelagians. It also made it possible for Augustine's teaching to embrace the scriptural assertion that God willed *all* to be saved.

Prosper continued to refine Augustine's views. He agreed that God's foreknowledge of someone's damnation was not the same thing as God's *desire* for that person's damnation. Rather, Prosper said, it was God's foreknowledge that such a person would *refuse* belief which motivated God to withhold the grace of salvation. This injected a certain rationale into Augustine's position, and undercut the criticism that Augustine had believed in salvation by blind chance.

As Prosper continued to emphasize God's foreknowledge rather than his predestination, the latter concept became less and less significant in the debate. Eventually Prosper did not even refer to the concept, focusing instead on the positive aspects of Augustine's teaching—namely, that grace is essential and that God desires all to be saved. (Prosper downplayed Augustine's more troubling corollary—"No one is saved unless God desires it.")

Given Prosper's effort to harmonize Semi-Pelagianism with Augustinianism, all that remained was for the Church to effectuate a reconciliation and to define it in an official formula of faith. Accordingly, at the Synod of Orange (in southern France) in 529, Abbot Caesarius of Arles (470-542) and the bishops in the area where the controversy had been centered resolved the controversy.

They supported Augustine's position by concluding that in Adam's fall all humanity had been injured—body and soul. Further, they vindicated Augustine's teachings that it is God who plants in the human soul the initial movement toward faith, that God's grace is prior to every human good work, and that humanity unassisted by grace is incapable of achieving salvation. Yet, the bishops nowhere referred to predestination in their *canons*. Following Abbot Caesarius's teaching they explicitly condemned anyone who professed a belief in damnation as God's will, quoting Augustine's own words: "When men do what is displeasing to God, they perform their own will, not God's."[15]

The Synod of Orange in effect proclaimed the vast bulk of Augustine's teaching to be orthodox. At the same time, in a subtle rejection of Augustine's more dubious propositions—particularly his views on predestination—the bishops simply affirmed the necessity and priority of grace in the Christian's movement toward salvation. They did not enter into the thorny controversy over how many will ultimately be saved.

The Synod of Orange thus preserved the core of Augustine's teaching without following that teaching to some of its more negative extremes. As if to assure everyone that they cast no aspersions on Augustine's authority, they condemned the teaching of Faustus of Riez. Pope Boniface II (530-532) confirmed the Synod's work when he wrote to Abbot Caesarius, "We approve your confession as in harmony with the catholic rules of the fathers."[16]

By establishing the core of Augustine's theology as its doctrinal foundation, the Western Church had prepared itself to move into the Middle Ages on unshakable intellectual footing. With the exception of the Apostle Paul, no other person was to have as great an influence on the future course of Western Christianity and civilization.

Little wonder that Augustine's contemporaries inscribed these words at the base of a statue bearing his likeness: "The different Fathers taught us various things; this man taught us everything."

Augustine's Place in History

We could not possibly have done justice to all of Augustine's thinking in this brief chapter. Because Augustine's theology of grace becomes so significant to both medieval and Reformation theology, we have emphasized Augustine's teaching in this area to the exclusion of, for example, his mystical and biblical writings.

If Augustine's views on grace are unsettling to our modern belief in the supremacy of the human will, perhaps we could try to place ourselves in his shoes: a man writing in extremely chaotic times, times in which the absolute majesty of God was placed in doubt by new currents of thought and new social forces. Could it be that Augustine's uncompromising teaching on "the sovereign grace of God" is something that our own age needs to hear and to accept?

CHAPTER TEN

SHAPING THE CHURCH

Ordinary Church Life on the Eve of the Middle Ages

Because history tends to be written in terms of big names and events, we can get the impression that life in the past was a constant recurrence of exciting and dramatic happenings. In reality, people in the past were like us in most respects. Their major concerns were their own daily lives—their families, homes, jobs and all the little things that no one ever finds interesting enough to record.

The people of the early Church are no exception. This gradual unfolding of ordinary events and circumstances played as great a role in shaping the early Church as did confrontations between bishops and the writings of famous theologians. We have already seen how local "rules of faith" consistently contributed to the formulation of the Creeds. And we have seen how the faith of ordinary people provided the touchstone for theological debate. Before we leave the early Church, let us take a brief look at some of the other less conspicuous goings-on which shaped the Church's character.

A CHANGING STRUCTURE: FROM 'CIRCLE' TO 'PYRAMID'

One of the most significant effects of Constantine's conversion was the gradual diversification of Christians into different ranks. When the Empire became the Church's official patron and protector, the Church began to adopt much of the Empire's administrative machinery. The Church more and more tended to model its governing structure on the

Empire's own hierarchical system of organization. Therefore, after the fourth century clergy and laity shared their lives less intimately than before.

Eventually the Church's organizational model came to mirror the Empire's own model—the pyramid. Authority was seen as centered in the apex of the pyramid and filtering down to the base. This model worked pretty well in a time when rigid bureaucracy was needed to give order and structure to a populous Christian society separated by both vast distances and vast differences in language and culture.

Before the fourth century, however, smaller, more homogenous local congregations had worked out a different organizational model: the circle. In this circle laity and clergy joined hands and looked to Christ at the center for guidance and leadership. As the Church became a more complex institution, the pyramid model replaced the circle.

The pyramid model of authority filled a need of the times for order, stability and certainty. One problem with the pyramid model, however, was that it came to be thought of not only as an *organizational* model, but as *the model* by which God operated in his Church. In time not only authority, but *grace* itself came to be seen as filtering down from above through the various hierarchical levels.

The laity was placed at the bottom of the pyramid not only as far as authority was concerned, but also in terms of its access to God's grace. By the Middle Ages the erroneous notion had developed that one could approach God only by going up the pyramid—up the hierarchy of the clergy. Ironically, the very Church which had defeated this same type of thinking in Gnosticism—with its extensive hierarchies of intermediaries (see p. 37)—eventually adopted virtually the same concept for its own everyday relationships. This is illustrated in the developing organization of clerical life during the last three centuries of the early Church.

The Ranks of the Clergy

By the fifth century the clergy had been subdivided into major categories: "superior clergy" and "inferior orders"—so called in a letter of Pope Innocent I (401-417). The former included bishops, priests and deacons; the latter included a whole new strata of offices: subdeacon, acolyte, exorcist, porter and lector.

Requirements for admission to the various ranks varied from place to place until the tenure of Pope Zosimus (417-418), who specified the period of time one had to remain at a particular level before advancing to the next. Zosimus also established minimum age requirements for admission to the various ranks. For example, a deacon had to be 25 years of age and a priest 30. (Although in the first three centuries the Church

140

had ordained deaconesses, by the fourth century the clerical ranks had become closed to women.)

Starting in the fourth century, the Church elaborated upon the qualities a man had to possess prior to his entry into clerical orders. Generally speaking, priests had to be without physical blemish or mental disorder, and had to have proven themselves morally upright. Usurers and anarchists, for example, were specifically prohibited from the clerical ranks. It was apparently Augustine who organized the first seminary for priestly education; prior to that time candidates for the priesthood received their training by studying as an apprentice under their local bishop.

Celibacy

The origins of *priestly celibacy* can be traced to the Spanish Synod of Elvira (c. 306) which required continence of all *married* clergy under pain of excommunication. How the Spanish bishops monitored the sexual conduct of married clergy is not known. Gradually, however, scrupulous clergy separated themselves from their wives in order to avoid the suspicion of unsettling behavior in the bedchamber.

The Spanish example spread to Italy. Pope Damasus instructed his priests to value spiritual fatherhood more greatly than physical fatherhood, urging the priests not to soil their "cultic purity" by sexual relations with women.

Pope Siricius expanded Damasus' teaching, decreeing that no married bishop, priest or deacon could continue sexual relations after ordination. Pope Innocent I ruled that monks (who already were bound by a vow of celibacy) could not be freed from their vows should they decide to seek ordination to the priesthood. In the East, Emperor Justinian prohibited married men from becoming bishops. A later Eastern council required Eastern *bishops* to separate from their wives. *Priests and deacons* in the East could remain married so long as they did not have sexual intercourse on days when they celebrated Mass.

In both East and West, individual bishops gradually required *prior* celibacy as a condition for ordination to the diaconate and priesthood. Nevertheless, the majority of bishops and priests were married as late as the seventh century.

Once again the Spanish Church led the way to modification of the common practice. The Fourth Council of Toledo in 633 required bishops and priests to take a vow of chastity. Gradually celibacy became the rule, and married clergy the exception. The Second Lateran Council of 1139 made the marriage of clerics unlawful and invalid.

When we look for the motives behind this rule of priestly

celibacy, we do not find the arguments commonly advanced today: that celibacy frees a man for more time to spread the gospel, that Jesus himself was unmarried, etc. Rather, it is sad to admit, the principal motive behind priestly celibacy was a growing belief that sexual intercourse somehow rendered persons less "spiritual" than persons who adhered to strict celibacy. It is this attitude which underlay Pope Damasus' remark concerning the priests' cultic purity. Not until the Middle Ages is a more studied theory of priestly celibacy developed.

The Clergy as a Separate Caste

Increasingly, clerics became a separate caste within society. Constantine exempted them from mandatory military and civil service, and Constantius exempted them from the burden of paying taxes. Bishops were established as judges competent to judge civil matters—and were eventually given offices within the imperial hierarchy. Bishops came to be called "most glorious" and priests and deacons "illustrious."

The bishops took over the dress and insignia of imperial officers, such as the pallium and stole. Priests too began to dress differently from lay people. Pope Gregory eventually decreed that all clerics must wear distinctive garb, though he did not prescribe what this should be.

A Developing Liturgical/Devotional Life

Baptism and Eucharist

The celebration of the various liturgies and the administration of the sacraments was the clergy's principal ministry. The various Christian congregations throughout the Empire knew slightly different forms for Baptism and the Eucharist. The following instructions of Hippolytus reveal the common third-century practice for ministers of the Eucharist to compose their prayers:

> It is not at all necessary for the bishop in giving thanks to recite the same words as we have given as if they were to be learned by heart. But let each pray according to his capacity. If he can pray in a long and solemn prayer, it is good. But if in his prayer he prays at modest length, no one may prevent him, provided only that his prayer is orthodox. [1]

Yet there was reliance everywhere on uniform prayers.

By the fifth century in the West, the form of the Eucharistic liturgy developed by the Roman Church had become more and more the norm. It wasn't until the time of Pope Damasus, however, that the Roman liturgy adopted the Latin language over the traditional Greek.

Baptism and Eucharist continued to be the principal sacraments. Penance, ordination, marriage and anointing of the sick were not recognized everywhere as sacraments. They were, however, universally regarded as *sacramental*—that is, they were understood to be means of grace.

The embarrassing practice of postponing baptism until death began to lose favor, and infant baptism slowly became the norm. As the place for baptism increasingly shifted from the cathedral's baptistry to the parish church, the Easter vigil ceased being the normal time for the rite of initiation. Most infants were now baptized at Christmas. In place of the catechumenate, *godparents* served as the means by which the young initiates learned the truths of the faith.

Penance

At the start of the fifth century, penance was still public, and official reconciliation was still the bishop's function. Eventually, owing to the ever-growing number of penitents (and the growing number of those who needed penance but put it off), the Roman bishops began to delegate the rite of reconciliation to priests.

The growing number of penitents mandated against the *public* nature of penance. In the sixth century Caesarius of Arles complained that most people were putting off penance until the time of death. Such criticism led to a reevaluation of public penance.

Once again the Spanish Church was the innovator and, in the sixth century, developed *private* penance. Abbot Columban (c. 543-615) of Ireland adopted the Spanish practice and, through his missionary monks, private penance spread to the continent.

POPULAR PIETY

The laity needed no instruction from the clergy in developing its own style of piety. Yet the preaching of bishops and priests served to mold and direct that piety. The core of the Church's preaching was Christ and the Scriptures. Formal prayer became more and more directed to Christ; over and over again the ordinary Christian was exhorted to study the Gospels and to pattern his or her life on that of the Savior.

With the end of persecution and the decline of martyrdom, Christians began to express their admiration for the great heroes of the faith by making pilgrimages to the famous locales of persecution and by bringing back relics of the martyr's body or clothing. The idea developed that one could ask the departed martyr's intercession before God for earthly requests. Soon this practice was extended to holy men and women who had not been martyred but whose presence in heaven could be assumed because of their great reputation for holiness. The list of these "saints" thus grew to encompass non-martyrs such as Anthony, Athanasius, Basil, Ambrose and Augustine.

Beyond question, however, the saint of saints in the popular mind was the Virgin Mary. Both Ambrose and Augustine gave Marian devotion a solid doctrinal footing. Her perpetual virginity had been defended by Irenaeus, Clement and Athanasius. Bishop Gregory of Tours (c. 540-594) clarified the centuries-old tradition which held that Mary had been assumed bodily into heaven. And in the sixth century the feast of the Assumption entered liturgical calendars throughout the Church.

THE LAITY IN TRANSITION

As the early Church became more stratified into clergy and laity, it commonly became assumed that holiness also apportioned itself hierarchically: The further up the pyramid, the greater access to holiness. While many of the clergy promoted the priesthood of all believers, as well as the dignity of the lay apostolate, the laity's previous service to the Church was increasingly taken over by clerics. Irenaeus had written that "all the righteous have a priestly order," and "all the disciples of the Lord are Levites and priests."

The fourth-century Synod of Laodicea prescribed the seating arrangements to be observed in churches, decreeing that the laity be placed in the body of the church separated by a railing from the clergy who sat in the front. In the East a curtain separated "the crowd" from the priest, who celebrated the liturgy by whispering the prayers of consecration inaudibly.

In both East and West the laity was constrained against any type of participation in the Mass. The Eucharist came to be seen more and more as the priest's act of intercession *on behalf of* the people, rather than as the entire Church's act of thanksgiving. The consecrated bread became less the focus of a communal meal and more a venerated object.

The Church's teaching function—which in the earliest days had been the prerogative of lay persons such as Justin Martyr, Tertullian, Clement of Alexandria and Origen (in his early days)—now became the sole duty of clerics. Pope Leo I expressly prohibited lay people from teaching.

By the seventh century the chief importance of the laity lay in its financial support of the clergy, in its (decreasing) administration of Church property, and in its advancement of the Church's interests before the civil authorities. As the calling of the unordained Christian became increasingly less honored, men and women who sensed in their hearts the gospel's call to commit their lives totally to Jesus Christ developed an alternative to both the ordained and married states.

MONASTICISM

Next to the Creeds, the greatest achievement of the early Church was monasticism. The Christian form of this universal religious phenomenon came into existence for several reasons. A key factor was the desire for a life of greater holiness outside of the confines of ordained ministry. (Monks and, of course, nuns were not ordained.) Related to this was the wish to imitate the martyrs' total commitment to the gospel in a time when martyrdom itself had ceased. Overriding both of these factors, however, is the central ingredient of monastic life, both in the early Church and now: the desire to find God in the depths of one's inner being and to attune one's own spirit to God's indwelling Spirit.

Monasticism then and now is the most inexplicable of Christian life-styles. Even today there is no practical answer to the question, "Why would anyone want to become a monk (or a cloistered nun)?" In the last analysis there isn't anything practical about monasticism, just as there isn't anything practical about dying on a cross. Attempts to justify monasticism in terms of the "good works" monks perform for society—their cheeses, jellies, dairy farms, scientific and literary advances—miss the mark. Anyone who has lived in a monastery knows that such accomplishments are essentially frivolous in comparison to the monk's real work, to become transformed into a single-hearted lover of God.

Likewise, every monk has experienced the falsehood of the most common criticism of the monastic life—that it is merely an escape from the world's harsh realities. There is no less escapist vocation than monasticism. In the silence and solitude of the monastery one finds all the world's evils magnified within one's own soul.

Every Christian in a sense is called to be a monk, even *in* the world. Yet the Christian's unswerving commitment to Jesus is sometimes contradicted by the world's call to money, fame and power. It is precisely when the soul has suffered a surfeit of these commodities that it yearns for the monastic life, whether such a life is experienced as a permanent commitment to a cloistered order or through daily injection of the monastic spirit into one's life through regular silent prayer and deep meditation on the Scriptures.

Christian monasticism sprang from this desire for *God alone* that is implanted in everyone's heart by the Creator. The origins of Christian monasticism thus lie not so much in various historical circumstances as in the realization deep within the human heart, as Augustine phrased it, that "our hearts are restless, O God, until they rest in you."

Desert Hermits
Christian monasticism first took on an organizational identity in Egypt in the late third century. A young Egyptian hermit named Anthony was the first to draw followers to himself in a significant way. Athanasius had lived with this great desert father, and in his *Life of Anthony*, Athanasius greatly popularized the monastic calling in East and West.

Among the wealthy classes in the fourth century it became as common to have visited a notable desert saint as it was fashionable in America during the 1970's to have studied under an Indian guru. Yet, Anthony and his fellow hermits lived heroic lives which ordinary Christians could not truly emulate. Another Egyptian organized monastic life so as to make it accessible to everyone.

Communal Models
Pachomius (c. 290-346) founded the first monastic *coenobium* (from the Greek for "common life") around the year 325. Men lived together under the authority of an abbot and in obedience to a written constitution called a *rule*. Pachomius's motto was "All should be a help to you, and you should be a help to all." He perceived correctly that only a very few could undergo great spiritual warfare alone, as in Anthony's system. Pachomius's monastic foundation at Tabennisi in upper Egypt proved so successful that within 50 years nine Pachomian monasteries for men and two for women grew up in Egypt. Thus was founded the first monastic *order*, or confederation of monasteries and convents submitted to the authority of an abbot-general and a common rule.

Almost simultaneously with the Pachomian experiment, monasteries took root in Syria (at Mt. Sinai, 380) and in Palestine. Palestinian monks congregated in *laura*, which differed somewhat from Pachomius's *coenobium*. In the *laura* the monks each had a separate cell, all of which were gathered around a central building containing the church. The monks of the *laura* worked in solitude and came together only for liturgical celebrations. In the *coenobium*, on the other hand, monks slept, ate and worshiped under one roof and worked together.

Exaggerated Asceticism
Syrian monasticism was known for its exaggerated mortification. Syrian monks often wore heavy chains around their waists and neglected food and sleep to the detriment of their health. One famous holy man,

Simeon the Elder (c. 390-459), lived for years in a hut on top of a pillar 60 feet in the air. Theodoret of Cyrrhus in his *History of the Monks* described the varieties of Syrian monasticism:

> Some struggle in community; there are many thousands of such monasteries; others choose the eremetical life and are intent on conversing with God alone. Others praise God while living in tents and huts, others still in holes and caves. Many...endure the hardships of the climate. Now they grow numb in the extreme cold, now they burn under the scorching rays of the sun. Some stand without interruption, others allot the day to sitting and praying. Some have enclosed themselves within walls and avoid contact with men, others renounce such seclusion and are accessible to all who want to see them.[2]

Exaggerated asceticism such as that described by Theodoret frequently led to unchristian behavior and beliefs. A group of monks known as Messalians (literally, "praying people") taught that only by contemplative prayer—to the exclusion of the ordinary sacramental life—could one exorcise an "inner demon" with which all people were born. The Messalians particularly avoided contact with the institutional Church. Such distortions of the monastic calling troubled many bishops, who began to wonder if monasticism was an unhealthy aberration within Christian life.

With Basil the Great, however, balance was restored, and the hierarchy's fears calmed. In his *Rule* (358-64), Basil defined more clearly than had Pachomius the steps required for a person's full acceptance into the monastic community. He thereby allowed undesirable fanatics to be screened out before they had seduced others to their abnormalities. Basil also strengthened the concept of abbatial authority and placed greater demands of obedience upon his monks. Finally, he specified that the monastery lay under the control and authority of the local bishop.

Western Monasticism

Western monasticism began in the East. Western Christians eager for a deeper spiritual life had listened to Athanasius and other Eastern Christians extol the virtues of monasticism. Many flocked eastward—usually to Palestine—to found Latin-speaking monasteries. Women were in the forefront of this movement. Melania the Elder left Rome in 372 and founded a monastery on Mount Olivet, the first Latin monastery on Palestinian soil.

Another Roman woman, Paula the Elder (347-404), the mother of five children, followed Jerome to Bethlehem and founded a monastery and a convent. When Paula died, her daughter and then her niece served as spiritual leaders of the community. A Roman couple, Melania and Pinian, after all their children had grown, founded the third Latin monastic settlement in Palestine.

The Latin monasteries in Palestine differed from their Greek counterparts in that they were constituted largely from the educated classes. Thus Western monasticism from its earliest days displayed an interest in erudition and learning. Augustine's community at Thagaste (see p. 127) continued this emphasis, although the great Benedict purposely selected only the humblest and least educated brothers for his own monastic community in Italy.

The first monastery in the West was of a new variety. Bishop Eusebius of Vercelli in 363 organized his priests into a *clerical monastery*, laying the foundation for the medieval "canons regular," or secular priests living together under a monastic rule. To the north Bishop Martin of Tours (d. 397) founded the first monastery in France, at Liguge, and promoted monasticism's spread throughout Europe by placing himself and his monks at the service of local churches for preaching and teaching.

About 50 years after Martin's foundation, a wealthy Frenchman named Honoratus (c. 350-429) founded the monastery at Lerins, which became the center for the Semi-Pelagian school (see p. 135). Lerins distinguished itself by attracting educated young noblemen to its cloister, and by producing nearly every significant French bishop of the day. Monasticism gradually became the leading spiritual influence on the European Church's life in the fifth and sixth centuries.

Benedict of Nursia

The greatest exponent of Western monasticism was Benedict of Nursia (c. 480-550), who first withdrew from Roman society at the turn of the sixth century and lived as a hermit in a cave at Subiaco. His sanctity became legendary. Practically without his knowing it, 12 monasteries branched off from his foundation. About the year 525 he started a new formation at Monte Cassino, where he wrote his famous *Rule*. He seems to have simply acquiesced to the demands of others in establishing the new Benedictine monastic order.

Benedict insisted on simplicity, and he selected the least affluent and educated of men to form his communities. Ironically, after his death, Benedictine houses became centers of great learning, where ancient classical writings and the Bible were preserved from complete destruction during the barbarian takeover of Roman civilization.

Benedict's sister, Scholastica, founded a convent not far from Monte Cassino, and the two spiritual giants regularly met to plot the direction of Western monasticism. They chose to be buried in the same grave.

Benedict's *Rule* has had as much influence on the course of Church history as any other ancient document. It cannot be adequately summarized, since it is meant to be understood through its daily implementation. Yet, its twin themes of the imitation of Christ and love of the brothers—the most lasting achievement of early Christian monasticism—are illustrated in this brief excerpt:

> Just as there exists an evil fervor, a bitter spirit, which divides us from God and leads us to hell, so there is a good fervor which sets us apart from our evil inclinations and leads us toward God and eternal life. Monks should put this fervor into practice with an overflowing love; that is, they should *surpass each other in mutual esteem*, accept their weaknesses, either of body or of behavior, with the utmost patience; and vie with each other in acceding to requests. No one should follow what he considers to be good for himself, but rather what seems good for another. They should display brotherly love in a chaste manner; fear God in a spirit of love; revere their abbot with a genuine and submissive affection. Let them put Christ before all else; and may he lead us all to everlasting life.[3]

With our discussion of monasticism, we have now reached the end of our survey of the early Christian epoch. We have considered all the great themes: the conflict between revelation and philosophy, the battle with heresy, the evolving Church-State tension, the formulation of the great Creeds. It is time now to see if we can make a conclusion about the early Church on the eve of the Middle Ages. In doing so we will consider the last Creed left to us by the People of the Creed.

CONCLUSION

The Evolution of Faith

A good summary of the Church's faith after its first five centuries of existence is found in a credal document known as the *Apostles' Creed*. Its sixth-century form reads as follows:

> I believe in God the Father almighty, Creator of heaven and earth; And in Jesus Christ, his only Son, our Lord, Who was conceived by the Holy Spirit, born from the Virgin Mary, suffered under Pontius Pilate, was crucified, dead and buried, descended to hell, on the third day rose again from the dead, ascended to heaven, sits at the right hand of God the Father almighty, thence He will come to judge the living and the dead; I believe in the Holy Spirit, the holy Catholic Church, the communion of saints, the remission of sins, the resurrection of the flesh, and eternal life. Amen. [1]

This Apostles' Creed, contrary to later legend, did not originate from the hands of the Apostles, but from a sixth-century Christian community in the area of today's Franco-Spanish border. It is a purely *Western* Creed. Notice the lack of philosophical concepts such as *homoousios*. Like the earliest rules of faith, the Apostles' Creed is more practical in nature. It was adopted by the Frankish kings as the norm of orthodoxy for all Christians in the Frankish empire.

By Charlemagne's time (ninth century), this Creed had become firmly implanted in the consciousness of pious believers as a constituent element of the Christian faith. It was repeated several times daily as a prayer and incorporated into the rite of the Mass.

By the 10th or 11th century, the Apostles' Creed had made its way across the Alps to Italy. It was adopted by the popes as the official Roman Catholic Creed, thereby supplanting the Western Church's previous usage of the Constantinopolitan Creed (C) of 381 (which was itself an elaboration of the Nicene Creed; see p. 63). It was not until recent years that the Roman liturgy restored C to a position of priority, reserving the Apostles' Creed for subsidiary usage.

Comparing the sixth-century Apostles' Creed (A) to the patriarch of the Christian Creeds, the second-century Roman rule of faith (R), provides an excellent means to gauge the evolution of Christian faith from post-apostolic times to the transition period between early and medieval Christianity. Notice in A the following significant additions to R (see text on p. 49):

1) "Creator of heaven and earth"
2) "*Conceived* by the Holy Spirit, *born* from the Virgin Mary"
3) "*Suffered* under Pontius Pilate"
4) "Descended to hell"
5) "Holy *Catholic* Church"
6) "The communion of saints"
7) "Eternal life"

Taken together, these additions lead us to two parallel conclusions about the early Church's developing faith: (1) The core Christian beliefs expressed in rudimentary form in R have not varied in four centuries. (2) Although great theological debates have molded the content of the faith, these debates have not altered that faith in any substantial way.

By the end of early Church history we see therefore that, while Christian thought may have influenced belief, belief is nonetheless the unalterable bedrock underlying Christian thought. This becomes clearer when we look closely at A's seven additions to R.

1) By adding "creator of heaven *and earth*" to its dogmatic formula, the sixth-century Church expresses the fruits of its victory over Gnosticism: God is creator not only of spirit but of *matter*. The good earth did not erupt by chance from the Gnostic pleroma's spontaneous emanation. God *purposefully* created the earth. The Church ultimately affirms Scripture's teaching, "God looked at everything he made and he found it very good" (Genesis 1:21).

2) By clarifying that Jesus is *conceived* of the Holy Spirit, the sixth-century Church avails itself of the wisdom gained during the Arian struggle. From the moment of his conception Jesus is divine. Mary, then, is *Theotokos*—Mother of God—as she brings Christ into the world. While R's wording allowed Subordinationists to argue that Jesus' human birth made him less than God, A's explicit distinction between the respective roles of the Holy Spirit and the Virgin dissolves the ambiguity.

3) By specifying that Jesus "suffered" under Pontius Pilate, A erases any trace of a *Docetic* understanding of Jesus' passion and death. Jesus was truly a man and truly suffered, contrary to the Gnostic/Docetic heresy which denied his full humanity.

4) Through the words "descended to hell," A adds to the Church's dogmatic formulation a statement about Christ's *salvific action*. Notice that neither R nor C (p. 79) explicitly states the *consequences* of Jesus' death and resurrection. A, by adding the detail of Christ's "descent," clarifies the Church's belief in Jesus' liberation of the souls who had been imprisoned by Satan. By this addition the Church aligns itself with Scripture's own words, "*Now* will this world's prince be driven out" (John 12:31).

5) With the preservation of "Catholic" in the phrase "holy Catholic Church" (already added to R by C in 381), the Church affirms two beliefs: (1) The Church is catholic, with a little "c," in the sense that it is universal in time and place. (2) The Christian Church is Catholic, with a capital "C," in the sense that it alone possesses the truths of faith in opposition to heretical sects such as the Donatists.

As early as the second century this latter understanding of "Catholic" is well attested. Even the pagan Celsus referred to the Catholic Church as the embodiment of orthodoxy. And the martyr Pionius, when asked what he called himself, replied, "A Christian," and when asked to what Church he belonged answered, "To the Catholic Church."[2]

6) By adding to R the phrase "communion of saints," A formalizes another important aspect of the sixth-century Church's belief—that all Christians living and dead are united in a bond of fellowship that cannot be broken. Bishop Nicetas of Remesiana (d. 414) is one of the first witnesses to this fundamental principle of the Church's self-image when he writes:

> What is the Church, but the congregation of all saints? From the beginning of the world patriarchs, prophets, martyrs, and all other righteous men who have lived or are now alive, or shall live in time to come, comprise the Church, since they have been sanctified by one faith and manner of life and sealed by one Spirit and so made one body, of which Christ is declared to be head, as the Scripture says. Moreover, the angels, and the heavenly virtues and powers too, are banded together in this Church...So you believe that in this Church you will attain to the communion of saints.[3]

7) Finally, by adding the words "eternal life" to R's formula, A clarified the Church's understanding of the resurrection. This was necessary in order to calm the doubts of some believers who, since the

fifth century, had come to misunderstand the distinction between Jesus' *resurrection* and Lazarus's *resuscitation* (John 11:1-44). By specifying that all Christians possess "eternal life," the Apostles' Creed affirms Christianity's belief in the immortality of the resurrected and glorified body. On their deaths, Christians will never die again, as Lazarus did. Rather, they live forever, possessed of the same glory as the risen Jesus himself.

END OF AN ERA

This comparison of A and R shows that, aside from a few "mid-course corrections," the Church on the eve of the Middle Ages was following the same course as plotted by the Apostles themselves. Though riven at times by tumultuous storms, the "bark of salvation" continued its passage substantially on course.

In making this passage, the great formulas served as a bridge for the transmission of normative Christian faith from the early Church to the medieval Church. The era of the Creeds has ended. These great expressions of a people's faith have served their purpose. The "People of the Creed" have become the "People of the Faith."

NOTES

Chapter One

1. "Letter of Clement to the Corinthians," 45, *Early Christian Writings* (Penguin Books, 1968), p. 45.
2. *Ibid.*
3. "Letter of Ignatius to the Trallians," 2, *Early Christian Writings*, p. 96.
4. *Ibid.*, 3.
5. Irenaeus, "Fragments," 33, *The Emergence of the Catholic Tradition*, J. Pelikan (University of Chicago Press, 1971), p. 164.
6. Clement of Alexandria, "The Tutor," 1.6.26.1-2, *ibid.*
7. Cyprian of Carthage, "Epistles," 74.5, *ibid.*, p. 166.
8. Irenaeus, "Against Heresies," 4.18.5, *ibid.*, p. 167.
9. Ignatius, "Letter to the Smyrneans," 7, *Early Christian Writings*, p. 121.
10. Ignatius, "Letter to the Ephesians," 20, *ibid.*, p. 82.
11. Justin Martyr, "First Apology," 66.2, *A History of Christian Thought*, J. L. Gonzalez (Abingdon Press, 1983), p. 109.
12. Here we follow H. Jedin, ed., *History of the Church* (Crossroad-Seabury Press, 1982), vol. I, pp. 281-285.
13. Hermas, "Mandates," 4.3.6, Gonzalez, p. 88.
14. "The Martyrdom of Polycarp," *Early Christian Writings*, pp. 158-159.
15. *Ibid.*, p. 162.
16. Eusebius, "Life of Constantine," Jedin, p. 425.

Chapter Two

1. Plutarch, "De Iside et Oriside," 78, *A History of Philosophy*, F. Copleston, S.J. (Image Books, 1962), Vol. I, Part II, p. 197.
2. Justin, "Dialogue With Trypho," Jedin, vol. I, p. 174.
3. Justin, "Dialogue With Trypho," 56.11, Gonzalez, p. 108.
4. *Ibid.*
5. Athenagoras, "A Plea for the Christians," 10, *ibid.*, p. 115.
6. Tertullian, "Prescription Against Heretics," *ibid.*, p. 179.
7. Clement, "Exhortation to the Greeks," 4.63.3, Pelikan, p. 36.
8. Origen, "Commentary on the Gospel of John," 13.46, Jedin, vol. I, p. 236.
9. Origen, "Against Celsus," 5.18-19, Pelikan, p. 48.
10. *Ibid.*, 5.23.
11. Celsus, quoted by Origen in "Against Celsus," 2:253-254, *ibid.*, p. 29.
12. Origen, "Against Celsus," 6.8, *ibid.*

Chapter Three

1. Irenaeus, "Against Heresies," 5.16.2-3, Pelikan, p. 144.
2. Tertullian, "Against Marcion," 1.19.4, *ibid*,. p. 74.
3. Irenaeus, "Against Heresies," 1.27.2, *ibid*.
4. Tertullian, "Against Marcion," 1.19.4, *ibid*., p. 72.
5. Irenaeus, "Against Heresies," 3.13.1, *ibid*., p. 113.
6. *Ibid*., p. 114.
7. Origen, "On First Principles," pr. 4, *ibid*., p. 117.
8. From J.N.D. Kelly, *Early Christian Creeds* (3rd ed.), 114 (David McKay Company, Inc., 1972).

Chapter Four

1. Eusebius, "Life of Constantine," 2.28, Jedin, vol II, p. 4.
2. *Ibid*., I, 44, 1-2, p. 81.
3. Sozomen, "Church History," 1, 15, 4, *ibid*., p. 17.
4. From H. Chadwick, "The Early Church" (Penguin Books, 1967), p. 124.
5. Arius, "Letter to Eusebius," 5, Pelikan, p. 193.
6. From Kelly, p. 183.
7. *Ibid*., p. 182.
8. *Ibid*., pp. 215-216.
9. Eusebius, "Letter," *ibid*., p. 249.
10. Athanasius, "History of Arianism," 42, *ibid*., p. 251.
11. Amphilochius, "Fragments," 16, Pelikan, pp. 204-205.

Chapter Five

1. From Kelly, pp. 293-294.
2. Jerome, "Against Lucifer," 14, *ibid*., pp. 292-293.
3. Theodoret of Cyrrhus, "Church History," 3.25, 6-7, Jedin, vol. II, p. 59.
4. Clement of Alexandria, "Exhortation to the Greeks," 1.8.4, Pelikan, p. 155.
5. Athanasius, "Against the Heathens," 40.4-5, Gonzalez, p. 303.
6. Amphilochius, "Synodical Epistle," Pelikan, p. 211.
7. Basil the Great, "Epistles," 38.5, *ibid*., pp. 219-220.
8. Basil the Great, "On the Holy Spirit," 9.23, *ibid*., p. 216.
9. Gregory of Nyssa, "There Are Not Three Gods," *ibid*., p. 223.
10. Theodosius I, *Cunctos Populos*," Jedin, vol. II, p. 68.
11. Gregory of Nazianzus, "Letter to Uedonius," Kelly, p. 307.
12. From Kelly, p. 297.
13. Athanasius, "Letters to Serapion," 1.31, *ibid*., p. 342.

Chapter Six

1. Attributed to Eudoxius of Constantinople, as in Jedin, vol. II, p. 93.
2. Athanasius, "Orations Against the Arians," 1.8, Pelikan, pp. 226-227.
3. *Ibid.*, 3.32, p. 248.
4. Gregory of Nazianzus, "Epistles," 101, Gonzalez, p. 360.
5. Theodore of Mopsuestia, "Exposition of Ephesians," Pelikan, p. 244.
6. Pope Leo the Great, "Tome," 4, *ibid.*, p. 245.
7. Theodore of Mopsuestia, "Catechetical Homilies," 4.6, *ibid.*, pp. 229-230.
8. Cyril of Alexandria, "On the Incarnation of the Only-Begotten," *ibid.*, p. 249.
9. Nestorius, "Fragments," 256, *ibid.*, p. 252.
10. Gustavo Gutierrez, "To Defend Life Is Subversive," *Maryknoll* (December, 1984), p. 42.

Chapter Seven

1. Theodoret of Cyrrhus, "Formulary," Chadwick, p. 199.
2. Leo the Great, "Sermons," 54.4, Pelikan, pp. 257-258.
3. *Ibid.*, "Tome," 3, p. 259.
4. Leo the Great, "Epistles," 4, Gonzalez, p. 384.
5. "Acts of the Ecumenical Council," II, 1, 2, 126-130, *ibid.*, pp. 390-391.
6. Pelikan, p. 267.
7. "Acts of the Second Council of Constantinople," Anathemas, 3, *ibid.*, p. 277.

Chapter Eight

1. Athanasius, "History of the Arians," 41, Jedin, vol. II, p. 83.
2. Ambrose, "Letters," 20, 19, *Social Thought*, Message of the Fathers of the Church, Peter C. Phan (Michael Glazier, Inc., 1984), vol. 20, p. 183.
3. *Ibid.*, "Sermon Against Auxentius," 36, p. 165.
4. *Ibid.*, "On Duties," III, 4, 25, p. 162.
5. *Ibid.*, "On Naboth," pp. 162-163.
6. Jerome, "Letters," 130, 14, *ibid.*, p. 187.
7. Augustine, "Commentary on Psalm 147," 12, *ibid.*, p. 197.
8. Jerome, "Life of St. Malchion," 1, Jedin, p. 90.
9. Irenaeus, "Against Heresies," 3, 3, 2, *ibid.*, vol. I, p. 356.
10. Cyprian, "On Church Unity," 4, *ibid.*, p. 359.
11. Cyprian, "On Church Unity," 4, Pelikan, p. 119.
12. Cyprian, "On Church Unity," 5, Gonzalez, p. 249.
13. Gregory the Great, "Epistles," 5.37, Pelikan, p. 352.

Chapter Nine

1. Augustine, "Confessions," 5, 6, Gonzalez, vol. II, p. 18.
2. *Ibid.*, 8. 12, p. 20.
3. *Ibid.*, "On the Trinity," 4. 21. 30, vol. I, p. 338.
4. *Ibid.*
5. *Ibid.*, 6. 5. 7, p. 341.
6. *Ibid.*, 6. 7. 9, p. 339.
7. Augustine, "Against Parmenian's Epistle," 1, 2, 3, Jedin, vol. II, p. 144.
8. Augustine, "On Baptism Against the Donatists," 7.53.102, Pelikan, p. 311.
9. From Jedin, vol. II, p. 151.
10. Synod of Carthage, "Canon," Pelikan, p. 318.
11. Augustine, "On the Predestination of the Saints," 5.10, *ibid.*, p. 329.
12. John Cassian, "Conferences," 13.8, Gonzalez, vol. II, p. 56.
13. *Ibid.*, 13.7, Pelikan, p. 322.
14. Prosper of Aquitaine, "Response to the Objections of the Gauls," 1.8, *ibid.*, p. 326.
15. Augustine, "Exposition of the Gospel of John," 19.19, *ibid.*, p. 327.
16. Boniface II, "Letter to Caesarius of Arles," *ibid.*, p. 329.

Chapter Ten

1. Hippolytus, "Apostolic Tradition," Chadwick, p. 263.
2. Theodoret of Cyrrhus, "History of the Monks," 37, Jedin, vol. II, p. 363.
3. "Rule of St. Benedict," Prologue, *The Liturgy of the Hours* (Catholic Book Publishing Co., 1975), vol. III, p. 1529.

Conclusion

1. From Kelly, p. 369.
2. Origen, "Against Celsus" and "The Martyrdom of Pionius," *ibid.*, p. 385.
3. Nicetas of Remesiana, "Explanation of the Creed," 10, *ibid.*, p. 391.

GLOSSARY

Adoptionism   A type of Monarchianism which taught that at some point in Jesus' life, such as his Baptism in the Jordan, God "adopted" Jesus by giving him divine power. This school of thought saw Christ as merely a man, but a man "permeated," as it were, with God's power. (Also known as Dynamic Monarchianism.)

aeons   In Gnosticism, lesser dieties that produced material creation and inhabited and ruled their own realms of existence.

Apollinarism   Extreme *logos-flesh* Christology advanced by Bishop Apollinaris of Laodicea which held that, while Christ had a human body, he had no human spirit. He was thus not truly a man.

apology   From the Greek word *apologia*, referring to a written defense of one's beliefs or position.

archons   (See **demiurge**.)

apostate   One who renounced the faith in time of persecution.

Arianism   A heresy preached by Arius toward the end of the third century and into the fourth which stressed that the Son (Jesus) is not of the same substance (*homoousios*) as the Father, but was created as a means for God to shape the world (a form of Platonism). The Arians could not conceive of a God in three persons who was at the same time the monotheistic God of Scripture, nor could they believe that the supreme, absolute God actually became human in Jesus. They referred to Jesus as a "lesser god." Arius said that the Son is not equal in divinity to the Father, a teaching which provided the impetus for the Council of Nicaea in 325.

canon   From the Greek for "measuring rod"; has come to mean norm or rule.

catechumen   A prospective convert to Christianity; the name given to a person seeking Baptism.

catechumenate   A lengthy period of instruction required prior to Baptism.

Christology   The study of Christ's person, focusing particularly on the union between his divine and human natures.

Christology, *logos-flesh*   Supported the belief that the eternal Word (Logos) was united only to Jesus' flesh (or body), and not to his entire person—body and *soul* (which for the ancients was somewhat similar to our concept of *mind*). Thus Jesus was believed to be "a man in whom God's mind operated." When pushed to its extreme form this Christology denied that Jesus really grew and matured in wisdom and understanding or that he really suffered temptations or other human psychological conflicts. (See also **Apollinarism** and **Monophysitism.**)

Christology, *logos-man* Supported the belief that the divine Word (Logos) was united to a *man*, not just to "flesh." In extreme form this school tended to deemphasize the divinity of Jesus, seeing him as a "god-filled man," rather than as true God and true man. (See also **Nestorianism.**)

communicatio idiomatum Latin phrase, meaning "communication of properties." A doctrine advanced especially by Bishop Cyril of Alexandria, maintaining that, because Christ's human and divine natures are united in the one person of Christ, what we can say about one nature can be likewise attributed to the other nature.

demiurge Used in Platonism to refer to an intermediary, lesser god that composed material creation (the "creator-god"). In Gnosticism the word refers to the evil god (creator of the material universe) which carried out the process by which the supreme God's fullness slipped away from him. In several Gnostic systems the demiurge is equated with the Jewish God, Yahweh, who created six vassal lords to serve him. These are called *archons* who, in turn, decided to "make man after *our* own image."

Didache Greek word for "teaching." An early second-century Christian writing describing important elements of worship and belief.

Didascalia A Syrian writing (c. 220) which, among other things, gives a detailed picture of the Eastern Church's requirements for post-baptismal penance.

Docetism From the Greek work for "appear," a heresy which stressed that Christ only *seemed* to have a human body and to suffer and die on the cross.

Donatism This distorted teaching on the *means* of grace was first proposed by Donatus (c. 311) in Northern Africa. It holds that the sanctity of the minister is essential for the valid administration of the sacraments. Donatus said that bishops who cooperated with the Romans during the persecutions had lost their baptismal holiness and thus could not validly administer the sacraments or validly ordain priests.

dualism A metaphysical system which held that God and the world are separate. Also, the Gnostic doctrine that the universe is under the dominion of two opposing principles, one of which is good and the other evil. (See also **monism**.)

Dynamic Monarchianism (See **Adoptionism**.)

ex opere operantis Latin phrase meaning "based on the person performing the action." Refers to the Donatist belief that the sacraments were only valid on the basis of the sacramental minister's personal holiness.

ex opere operato Latin phrase meaning "based on the action itself." Used to define the Catholic belief that the validity of a sacrament depends not on the minister, but on Christ himself who works through the minister.

Filioque From Latin, meaning "and the Son." Refers to the formula added to the Creed of Constantinople (381) by the Western Church to express the belief in the "double procession" of the Holy Spirit from the Father and the Son, rather than from the Father only, as the Creed had originally stated.

Formula of Union   A compromise statement drafted by Bishop Theodoret of Cyrrhus in 433 which temporarily ended the doctrinal quarrel between Alexandria and Antioch by declaring Christ to be "perfect man consisting of rational soul and body, of one substance with us in his manhood, so that there is a union of two natures; on which ground we confess Christ to be one, and Mary to be mother of God."

gnosis   (See **Gnosticism**.)

Gnosticism   A perverted version of Platonism based on the conviction that matter is evil and that salvation comes through *gnosis* (a secret "knowledge"). In the Gnostic system Christ was not the divine Son but a "messenger" who delivered the secret means to enlightenment.

heresy   An opinion or doctrine contrary to orthodox Christian belief.

homoiousios   "Of *like* substance," a term used to counter the suspicion that a similar Greek word, *homoousios* (see below), blurred the distinction between Father and Son.

homoousios   Meaning "of the *same* substance," from the Greek words *homo* (same) and *ousia* (substance).

homoousios formula   The doctrinal expression used by the Council of Nicaea to state the Son's equal divinity with the Father (theologically called "the homoousion"). In today's Creed it is translated ". . . *one in being* with the Father."

hypostasis   Greek word literally meaning "substance," but frequently understood also to mean "nature" or "essence." By the mid-fourth century it was being used for "person," so that a great deal of confusion resulted when writers applied the word to the three persons of the Trinity (i.e., did the word connote that the Trinity was God in three persons or God in three substances?).

hypostatic union   Term used to express the Christian belief that in the one person of Jesus Christ a human and divine nature (*hypostasis*) are inseparably joined together, or that there is a "substantial union" of the divine and human natures in the one person of Christ.

incarnation   The Christian belief in the union of divinity with humanity in the one person Jesus Christ.

lapsi   Latin for "the lapsed ones." The general name for those Christians who cooperated with Roman authorities during persecution. (See also *libellatici, sacrificati*.)

libellatici   Latin nickname for those Christians who, under persecution, bribed Roman officials to sell them a *libellus* (see below; see also **lapsi**).

libellus   Latin word referring to a *certificate* issued to an individual during the time of Christian persecution to certify that the person had offered sacrifice to the Roman gods.

logos   Greek word for "word" or "reason." The Stoics used the word to refer to God as the controlling and creative principle within the universe. Christianity uses the word to refer to the second person of the Trinity, the eternally existing "Word of God."

Marcionism A heresy propagated by Marcion around 140, which taught that Jesus only *appeared* to be human and that the human body was evil. Marcion preached the existence of two Gods: the harsh creator-god, Yahweh, and the Supreme One who sent Jesus into the world. Marcion considered love, or grace, the means of salvation, and law but a means of servitude to Yahweh.

Modalism A type of Monarchianism teaching that the one God exhibits different *modes* of behavior—one mode being represented by the Father, another by the Son and the third by the Holy Spirit. Any distinctions in the Trinity are dependent upon how God wants to operate at a given time. The heresy disbelieves in three divine persons in one God. (Also known as Modalistic Monarchianism or Sabellianism, after the most famous early Modalist, Sabellius. See also **Patripassianism**.)

Modalistic Monarchianism (See **Modalism**.)

Monarchianism From the word *monarchy*, a doctrine emphasizing the unity of God to the exclusion of his individualized personhood. (See also **Adoptionism** and **Modalism**.)

monism A metaphysical system adhered to by the Stoics which held that everything was part of one and the same ultimate substance: God. (By contrast, see also **dualism**.)

Monophysitism An extreme expression of *logos-flesh* Christology teaching that Christ possessed only *one nature*—a divine nature which fully absorbed his human nature.

Nestorianism An extreme expression of *logos-man* Christology preached by Nestorius and condemned by the Council of Ephesus in 431. Nestorianism held that the divine and human persons remained separate in the incarnate Christ. Following the Council of Ephesus, Nestorianism slowly began to emerge as the first separate Eastern Christian Church, centering in Persia and surviving today chiefly in Asia Minor.

Patripassianism Nickname given to a form of Modalism which stressed that the Father and Son were so completely united in the Godhead that it was accurate to speak of the Father as having died on the cross. The word literally refers to the belief that "the father suffers."

Pelagianism A heresy preached by Pelagius in the late fourth and early fifth centuries. Pelagius believed that all the grace humanity ever needed was released into the world at creation. This "grace of creation" was available to anyone who asserted his or her free will in the direction of good. Thus, one's freely chosen decision unaided by God's grace is the first step toward salvation, and everyone has the capacity to take this step. Pelagianism was condemned when Pelagius denied that an unbaptized person who performed good works was excluded from heaven. (See also **Semi-Pelagianism**.)

Platonism   The philosophy of Plato stressing especially that actual things are copies of transcendent ideas and that these ideas are the objects of true knowledge apprehended by reminiscence. Plato's philosophy greatly influenced early Christian thinking. Plato believed God and the world to be separate. God was the absolute and ultimate transcendent reality, above and beyond the world of the senses. In order to "arrange" the world (Plato did not believe in creation from nothing) and to sustain it, God employs a "craftsman" known as the *demiurge,* a "lesser-god." Platonism greatly influenced the heretical impulses within early Christian thinking which tried to keep God and his creation, spirit and matter, separate.

pleroma   A Greek word in Gnosticism referring to God's divine fullness.

pneuma   Greek for "spirit." In Gnosticism, the supreme God's divine spirit.

pneumatology   The theology of the Holy Spirit.

Pneumatomachians   Literally, "those who war against the Spirit." These heretics denied the divinity of the Holy Spirit. They were officially condemned at the Council of Constantinople in 381.

Rule of Faith   This phrase refers to short summaries of the core Christian belief which began to develop early in the second century in response to heresy. Every Christian congregation possessed its own "rule of faith" by which it expressed the essential truths of Christianity in ordinary everday language. These "rules of faith" were the forerunners of the great written Creeds.

Sabellianism   (See **Modalism**.)

sacrificati   Latin word used to refer to those Christians who actually sacrificed to the Roman gods during persecution. (See also *lapsi.*)

Semi-Pelagianism   A school of thought founded by Abbot John Cassian which tried to steer a middle course between Augustine's emphasis on grace to the exclusion of free will and Pelagius's emphasis on free will to the exclusion of grace.

Stoicism   A school of philosophy founded by Zeno of Citium about 300 B.C. holding that the wise person should be free from passion, unmoved by joy or grief, and submissive to natural law. This system of philosophy greatly influenced the Roman world and consequently Western civilization. For the Stoics the motivating force behind creation was the *logos.* This *logos,* which they defined as God the creator, was the actual "stuff" of God existing inside all matter. (See also **monism**.)

Subordinationism   The belief that the Son (Jesus) was "less divine" than the Father (God).

Theotokos   Greek for "God bearer." Used to define Mary as the "Mother of God" and accepted as an orthodox title for her at the Council of Ephesus in 431, as well as in the Formula of Union of 433 (see above).

traditor   From Latin, referring to a Christian who "handed over" Church books to the Roman police during the persecutions, hence the English "traitor."

INDEX